STILLWATER
☙ TROUT ❧

A Month-by-Month Guide

Brian Musgrove

BLANDFORD

A BLANDFORD BOOK
First published 1994
by Cassell
Villiers House
41/47 Strand
London
WC2N 5JE

Distributed in the United States
by Sterling Publishing Co., Inc.
387 Park Avenue South, New York, New York 10016-8810

Distributed in Australia
by Capricorn Link (Australia) Pty Ltd
2/13 Carrington Road, Castle Hill, NSW 2154

British Library Cataloguing-in-Publication Data
A catalogue record for this book is available
from the British Library

ISBN 0-7137-2438-2

Typeset by Method Limited, Epping, Essex, UK

Printed and bound in Finland

CONTENTS

INTRODUCTION

From the cold and windy sterility of early spring, through the long, hot dusty days of summer, and on to the ripening glories of a golden autumn – each part of the season poses its own unique problems for the bank angler. Our ability to recognize, prepare for and deal with these problems as they arise means, quite simply, the difference between success and failure.

It was with this thought in mind, and at the bequest of several of my fellow anglers, that I finally decided to put together a month by month guide which I hope will help you cope with the vagaries of an average season. In this book I also recommend sufficient fly patterns to carry you through the year. Some of these patterns you will know already, though you may not have fished them regularly, others have come (via my imagination) from my own fly box.

Anyone who has read my work before will know that I believe in keeping things as simple as possible. So, I shall not be asking you to take anything on trust, and any claims I make will be supported with logical argument.

No single piece of written work has ever transformed a beginner into an expert or a poor angler into a good one. But it is my sincere belief that, after reading this book, your awareness and understanding of what goes on around you at the waterside will be much greater than before. If this is truly the case, you can look forward confidently to many happy and successful days ahead.

FISH DEPTH GUIDES

Predicting the behaviour of trout on a short-term basis is, quite frankly, almost impossible. There are just too many unpredictable factors such as daily weather conditions, water temperatures, fly hatches, etc. Indeed it would be a very brave angler (or a very stupid one) who tried to forecast with any accuracy what the quarry's actions might be 24 hours ahead.

There are, however, advantages to stepping back a little and looking at the season as a whole. It is then, I believe, that a pattern emerges that is of use to anglers.

For example, as spring develops into early summer, we can be pretty certain that the trout will spend more of their time near the surface. Then, with the arrival of the predominantly hot days of July and August, it is reasonable to expect trout to seek temporary refuge in the deeper water during daylight hours. And later, as autumn draws near, it's reasonable to expect renewed surface activity as water temperatures begin to cool.

The depth tables provided at the end of each month's advice are based upon these gradual seasonal changes. Obviously they should not be regarded as one hundred per cent accurate. But they *have* been designed to aid you on those days when the trout do not give away their position by showing themselves. A quick glance at that month's guide will suggest a depth at which, all things being equal, you are likely to find the majority of fish.

APRIL

GENERAL ADVICE

There are very few things we can predict accurately at the start of a new season. Perhaps the one exception to this rule is that we know, with some certainty, that most of the fish we'll be casting to during these early, chilly weeks of the year will be fresh stockies. That in itself should not be a cause for complaint – far from it. Fresh stock fish have certain patterns of behaviour that we anglers can rely upon, and believe me, that's useful.

For example, there can be no doubt that recently introduced stock fish seem to enjoy each other's company. If you are able to find one or two the odds are you'll have found a shoal. But be warned – fresh stock fish don't just shoal, they shoal *tight!* This is particularly true of rainbow trout. A mere ten yards can mean the difference between being 'on fish' and being 'off'.

Another most endearing habit as far as the bank angler is concerned is the fish's preference for remaining close in for the first week or two after stocking has taken place. At this time of year I find I rarely need to lay more than twenty yards of line on the water. This apparently peculiar behaviour is in fact quite logical when you remember that, until recently, these fish will have lived in a stock pond with hundreds of others. The pond would have had clearly defined geographical boundaries and the fish it contained would have become conditioned to that sort of environment. Under those circumstances is it any wonder that, after being transferred to the main fishery, they continue to seek each other's company and shun the open water for what they consider the security of the bank?

At the beginning of a new season one principle should be kept at the forefront of the angler's mind and that is, with the exception of larger solitary fish, trout are essentially shoal creatures, primitive yet incredibly sensitive to the behaviour patterns of the rest of the shoal. Perhaps I should stress at this point that when referring to a 'shoal' I don't necessarily mean a huge gathering. A shoal can be as little as a dozen fish.

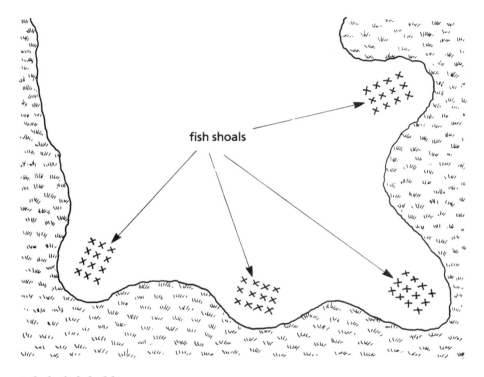

fish shoals

Likely fish-holding areas.

Shoal Feeding

My own observations and experience have led me to believe that feeding
is usually initiated in one of two ways.

1. The shoal will drift fairly inactively until it comes across a source of
   food. One or two fish then begin to feed and the rest, sensing what is
   happening, join in. The food source is not usually sufficient to
   sustain prolonged feeding in April but, while the food is available,
   the fish will compete for what is on offer. For this sort of brief
   activity it is essential that the angler be in the right place in order to
   make the most of it.

2. Hunger drives a minority of fish in the shoal to search more actively
   for food and, once again, this is communicated, triggering off a
   similar response in the remainder. These fish are not feeding in the
   truest sense but are 'up and looking' and will almost always come to
   the angler's fly. It is interesting to note that these periods of activity
   often last longer than a proper rise to a meagre fly hatch. These

searching fish don't usually stay in one place for very long. There are, however, some stretches of bank that seem more favoured than others, particularly narrow, shallow bays that must resemble their original stock-pond home.

Tactics

So, how do we set about catching these 'close-in' fish? The angler's initial task is, of course, to find them and for that we will need sharp eyesight, sound hearing and a sturdy pair of legs. To stick in one place for too long is a mistake unless there are obvious signs of fish activity. We would do better to take a leaf from the trout's book and keep searching. Rainbows in particular are creatures of extravagant behaviour. When they become active they'll show you where they are with the odd splashy rise or by rolling on the surface, and when one or two reveal themselves in this fashion you can near enough guarantee there will be more in the vicinity.

If April conditions are normal – and by that I mean cold, wet and windy – hatches of fly will be pretty scarce. There is bound to be the odd day when a few buzzers (Chironomid) put in an appearance and we could even see a few early olives, but generally the water will still be very cold and a prolific fly hatch is most unlikely. Consequently your choice of fly is probably less important now than at any other time of the year. Finding the fish, that's the hard part. Once found they're just as likely to take a white fly as a black one. My preferred early season patterns are a large Olive Nymph which I like to use when I can see fish in the upper water layers, and a Marabou Viva, size 8 or 10, which is a superb fly for fishing deep. I don't often go finer than a point of 5 lb breaking strain at this time of year. Fresh stock fish are not normally line shy.

When you find the trout you'll need to work fast. Don't cast to where you imagine the centre of the shoal to be. Drop your fly two yards the other side of them – give every fish a chance at it. Takes are usually pretty positive but don't wait to feel them. Watch your line for any unnatural movement, particularly in those first few seconds after the cast has been made when the fly is sinking slowly through the water. A trout can take the fly 'on the drop' and spit it out again – you'll never know it's happened if you wait to *feel* the take.

I said earlier that fly selection was not really that important in April and I meant it. However, the same cannot be said about the retrieve which, as always, is critical. Most of the standard artificials will catch fish for you providing they're presented properly. I usually start with a steady figure of eight but am always ready to try something different if the trout are not cooperating, and that really is the key to success. If you're covering fish that won't come to the fly by all means switch to another pattern. Just don't spend all day with your head inside your fly box! More often than not a change of retrieve will produce the desired results. Try speeding up, or slowing down. If they won't come to a

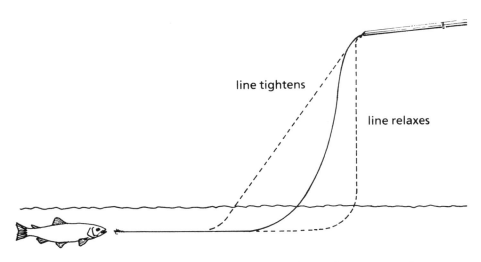

Watch the line from rod tip to water. Any sudden tightening or relaxing indicates a fish taking hold.

steady, continuous retrieve try short sharp pulls or a long slow sink and draw. Presentation is everything. The more tempting the fly's movements the higher your chances of success.

By the way, be aware that you'll need to alter the depth at which you're fishing fairly regularly to stay in contact with these stockies. They move up and down in the water almost as often as they move laterally.

Alternative Fishing

At almost all fisheries there are a number of over-wintered brown and rainbow trout that are the residue of last season's stocking and these are the fish I love to pursue during April. They are effectively wild fish and, unlike the stockies, rarely betray their position to the angler. Nevertheless, they are by no means impossible to catch. To find them will mean avoiding the more popular areas of bank-side for they are easily frightened. The stamping of wellington boots or careless wading is certain to spook them and so we need to adopt a much lower profile, a much more subtle approach altogether.

I like to begin by finding a relatively undisturbed stretch of bank, not the easiest of tasks in April, where the water is fairly shallow close in but drops away to fifteen or twenty feet a few yards out. My aim would be to fish the fly parallel with the bank just over the ledge where the shallow area drops away into deep water. If there are any over-wintered fish around they're likely to be cruising that ledge looking for the odd tasty morsel, knowing they have the security of deep water underneath them. Believe me, the slightest disturbance is likely to send them diving for cover.

For this kind of fishing I have found no better fly than the Cased Caddis. The caddis is the larval stage of the sedge fly (*Trichoptera*) and is something the fish will be expecting to find scuttling about on the bottom. These tiny creatures actually use materials from the lake bed to make little tube-like homes that they drag along behind them, only their head and legs visible. These tube cases offer a measure of protection against many other aquatic creatures but, unfortunately, none at all against the trout which gobble them up, house and all.

My objective from the start is to throw as long a line as possible parallel with the bank. I then allow plenty of time for the fly to sink to the ledge before beginning my retrieve, a very gentle pull of around six inches followed by a pause of two or three seconds. While retrieving I try to look down into the water with my mind's eye and imagine how my fly is behaving. First starting, then stopping to rest, then starting again. Moving . . . resting . . . tempting.

If there are any hungry trout in the vicinity they seem to find this kind of retrieve irresistible.

The takes, when they come, can be anything from a savage snatch that pulls the rod tip around, to the most delicate of offers that scarcely

Fishing the shelf for over-wintered fish.

moves the line at all. It is important when fishing the margins like this to stay on a floating line. Not only does it signal the delicate offers more clearly, it also allows the fly to be fished slowly without pulling it down into the debris on the bottom.

This 'alternative' early season fishing may seem to you a lot of trouble for little reward at this moment but, believe me, that feeling will only last until you have your first over-wintered fish on the bank. Then, if the fight hasn't taken your breath away, the condition of the fish will – fin perfect and with the bright firm flanks God intended the trout to have. Once seen, never forgotten!

Two Flies for April

Finding two flies I could recommend to you for April was one of the easier tasks I set myself in this book. We have already established that the angler's choice of fly early in the year is not yet of prime importance. So, on that basis, let's not begin by over-complicating things. All we really need are a couple of good general patterns, both with proven trout appeal and one with a little extra 'flash' to help provoke the right kind of response from the more reluctant fish. Here, in my opinion, are two of the best.

The Marabou Viva

My first nominated fly, the Marabou Viva, is one of the very best all-round lures. It will catch fish at any time of the year but is a particularly successful early season pattern. It is impossible to state with certainty why one lure should be more effective than another. I can only say in this case that the Viva combines two colours (black and bright green) that experience tell us are attractive to the trout. And of course marabou is a marvellously mobile material in the water. It really imparts life and movement to the fly.

How to Fish It
So, how should the Viva be fished? In a word, *slowly*! I cannot over-emphasize the importance of a steady retrieve when using marabou flies. A gentle figure of eight, or a slow pull and pause routine, really gives the feather a chance to work, producing that pulsing, eel-like wriggle that the trout seem to find irresistible.

All good flies have their strengths and weaknesses. I said earlier that the Viva will catch fish all year round, and so it will, but I believe it to be at its best when fished deep on those dour, early season days when nothing shows on the surface and sport is generally slow. Fishing then is largely an act of faith – faith in one's ability to sniff out the odd fish and, of course, faith in one's fly to tempt them when all around you are failing. Take it from me, the Viva is a fly you can put your trust in.

I tend to favour a slow sinking line with this pattern to start my season. It gives me maximum flexibility. A slow sinker takes the fly down on a fairly leisurely descent, giving fish at all depths plenty of time to inspect and grab hold if they're in the mood. And as a confirmed bank angler I know that most times I'll be casting into water no more than fifteen feet deep, so getting my flies down quickly isn't nearly as important as it would be for someone in a boat moored over depths of sixty feet.

Contrary to what some people might think, successful sunk line fishing requires a great deal of concentration. From the moment your fly disappears below the surface it is likely to be taken by a fish, and unless you're on your toes you won't even know it's happened! It is absolutely vital that the leader be straightened and the line tidied as soon as the cast has been made. Remember, give the fish no loose line to play with.

While waiting for the fly to reach the required depth watch the loop of line at your rod tip like a hawk and strike at any unusual movement, no matter how slight. You'd be surprised at how many offers are missed by anglers who wait for the rod tip to be pulled around by a taking fish. Use your fingers too. Feel for any change in line tension that might signify a trout interrupting the fly's descent.

Over the years I've lost count of the number of times when a dark and miserable day was brightened immeasurably by the sudden, electric 'snatch' that signals yet another trout has been deceived by that wicked black fly slinking across the lake bed, green tail winking seductively. Vive la Viva!

Tying Instructions

If you are a keen fly tier it won't take you long to realize that my instructions for tying some of the recognized fly patterns differ slightly from the original. This is due to the fact that either the material is no longer available (i.e. seal's fur), or quite simply that I believe my modifications produce a superior fly. If that sounds boastful or pretentious, I'm sorry. The truth is I've never been able to resist tinkering with the finished article. Now let's get back to tying the Viva.

HOOK: Partridge Grey Shadow Streamer, size 8/10.
BODY: Black seal's fur substitute.
TAIL: Fluorescent body wool (green).
RIB: Broad silver tinsel.
THREAD: Black.
WING: Black marabou.

Begin by laying down a neat bed of tying silk along the shank of the hook from eye to bend. Then layer on a little lead for ballast and tie in securely, returning the thread to the bend of the hook when you've finished. Fix the tail next, keeping it short and stubby, and catch in the silver ribbing while you're at it. Now dub on the SF substitute and build up a slim body, winding it back towards the eye of the hook. Follow this with the ribbing in nice even turns. All that's left now is the marabou wing which can be enhanced by a touch of black or copper Lureflash mobile. By the way, don't overdress the wing. Try to keep the fly as streamlined as possible.

The Standard Nymph

I once wrote, 'I cannot imagine a more beautiful sight than the steady take of a nymphing trout. There is a purpose and predictability about the whole sequence of events, a natural rhythm that allows a man time to savour the complete experience.'

That may sound a little flowery but it's exactly how I feel about Nymph fishing. I've been an angler since the age of seven, a fly fisher for more than half my life, and during that time nothing has given me greater pleasure than catching trout on Nymphs and other natural imitations. But learning to fish the Nymph well is not easy. There were many times during the early days of my apprenticeship when I was tempted to give up the struggle and revert to fishing the lure. The fact that I stuck it out, and even achieved a measure of expertise in the end, was due to nothing more noble than a bad case of pig-headedness on my part.

I did, however, learn a lot in those early days, such as the fact that the Nymph angler can be at something of a disadvantage in the first couple of months of the season when natural fly life is scarce. Fortunately it is nothing like as bad as some people make out. If the fish can be seen, and they're either feeding or in the mood to feed, then they'll take a Nymph nine times out of ten, even if they're fresh stockies that have never come across the real thing. The Nymph angler's problems only really begin when, for whatever reason, the trout make up their minds not to feed! In a situation like that most anglers, myself included, would offer the fish something large and colourful in the hope of provoking an aggressive response. Dedicated Nymphers on the other hand would rather leave the fish in the water than put up a lure. Now this may sound daft to some but it is the Nympher's pleasure and he should not be criticized for it.

If you are the angler faced with this dilemma what courses of action are open to you? You can keep on the move of course, hoping to find a few feeding fish – that's never a bad idea. Or you could simply hang about hoping for a hatch of naturals that might give your quarry a bit of a kick start, although there is an obvious drawback with that. As we've already discussed, hatches at this time of year are pretty scarce so you could be in for a long wait.

What to do? The advice I'm about to offer was born out of desperation on the kind of day we touched upon earlier, when, for prolonged periods, the fish simply refused to feed. I was pretty stiff necked in those days and stuck at it for hours, fishing my usual tiny Nymph patterns, never once persuading a trout to open its mouth. Finally, at the fag end of the day, I succumbed to temptation and switched to a lure. That belated move brought me three fish but did nothing for my temper. Those trout had found my small, rather dull patterns all too easy to ignore.

I'd love to say at this point that, in a sudden flash of inspiration, I solved the problem myself. Unfortunately that would not be true. The solution was offered to me on a plate when I met two other anglers (with whom I later became great friends) who showed me Nymphs at least twice the size of any I had in my fly box. With magnificently simple logic they deduced that if a large lure could generate an offer from a reluctant fish then so would a large Nymph. They were right!

I began tying my Standard Nymph pattern up to a size 8 and my catch rate rocketed. I can remember one day during that period bumping into Ken Giles, a regular member of England's coarse fishing team and a more than useful fly angler. He was having a particularly difficult day with the fish and, using tried and tested coarse angling logic, had scaled down to very small flies in the hope of scoring. I was doing very nicely with my 'monster' Nymphs a little further along the bank when Ken came to see me. I suggested he reversed his thinking and offered him one of my flies. Needless to say, he too was soon into fish.

My Standard Nymph has changed very little since those early days, the sign I suppose of a good fly. I have never been the kind of angler who, in order to save time, tackles up in the car park. I prefer to leave my line on the reel until I've had a look at the water. Mind you, if I was forced into making a premeditated choice of fly it would almost always be my Standard Nymph pattern. That's how much faith I have in its versatility.

How to Fish It

I really have very little to tell you with regard to how best to fish this fly. It is a Nymph and should be fished like a Nymph, with one important difference. When using it early season everything needs to be done a little quicker! If you're casting to fish on or near the surface do your best to see that the line and leader go down straight so that you're in a position to move the fly as soon as it has reached the required depth. Don't give the trout time to study it, that's the name of the game. Experience has taught me that the longer the fish spends looking the less likely it is to grab hold. The pace of the retrieve needs to be faster than normal too. Not lure stripping speed but roughly twice as fast as your usual figure of eight.

On occasions I have fished this pattern on a sinking line (and caught fish) but I much prefer to use it on floating or intermediate tackle in the upper water layers. The length and strength of leader should be dictated by the conditions and type of line used. I'm usually fairly happy with fifteen feet on my intermediate line and eighteen to twenty feet on my floater. By the way, a point of 5 lb breaking strain is fine for this kind of fishing. If the weather is very bright you may have to scale down to 4 lb but I wouldn't recommend anything lighter.

A great deal has been said and written about the art of presentation, particularly when fishing the Nymph. But in the end it all boils down to two things: depth and retrieve. The type and speed of retrieve you can experiment with until you click with the right method. The depth at which the fly should be fished, on the other hand, is not quite so easy to

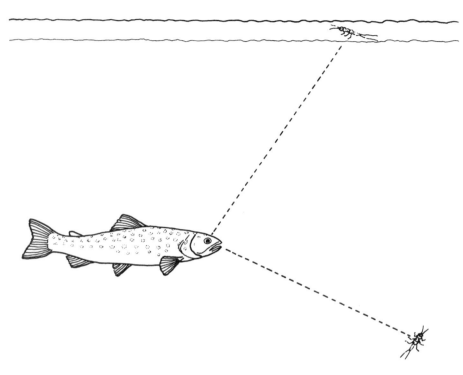

Trout searching for food often patrol four or five feet down. From there they are ideally situated to intercept any rising pupae while, at the same time, food trapped in the surface film can be easily seen.

fathom (please forgive the pun). All I can do is to suggest that you be guided by the number of fish you can see. If they're up on the top in quantity then that's where your fly should be. Conversely, if it is only the odd fish breaking the surface then be prepared to fish your fly four or five feet down. You could be in for a pleasant surprise. Trout searching for food often take up this position a few feet below the surface. From there they're ideally situated to intercept any rising pupae while, at the same time, food trapped in the surface film can be easily seen.

Tying Instructions

HOOK: Partridge Captain Hamilton H1A, size 14/12/10/8.
THREAD: Green.
BODY AND THORAX: A mixture of green and brown seal's fur or substitute.
RIB: Oval gold.
TAIL: Green cock hackle fibres.
HACKLE: Light green hen.
WING CASE: Pheasant tail.

Begin as always with a nice flat bed of tying thread. Then tie in just sufficient lead to help the fly turn over on the cast and to ensure it swims comfortably sub-surface. Only practice will tell you how much is enough. When the lead is tied in securely take the thread back down to the bend of the hook and tie in the tail and the ribbing. Before dubbing on the body of the fly take a pinch of at least two different shades of green body material, then add a pinch of brown and mix them thoroughly. Now dub this onto the thread and begin building up a slim body, working back towards the eye. The body of the fly should occupy approximately two-thirds of the hook shank. Follow this with the rib in smooth, open turns and tie off. The wing case comes next. Catch in a slip of pheasant tail feather by its tip, leaving the other end loose for the time being. Now dub on the thorax, not too heavy, and fix a sparse hackle. All that's left to be done then is the wing case. Fold the pheasant tail slip over the thorax and the hackle, tie off, and there you have it. By the way, after tying I always spend a few minutes plucking out a few body fibres. I like my Nymphs to look a little scruffy.

THINGS TO REMEMBER
⌘ APRIL ⌘

Water temperature   Low. Still feeling the effects of the rain and snows of winter.

Fly hatches   Sparse. An early hatch of buzzers is always possible at this time of the year but under normal circumstances little else can be expected until water temperatures begin to rise.

Fish behaviour   Most shoals will be made up of recently introduced trout. They will be very hungry. Competition between the fish for what is on offer will be high, which should ensure them coming quite boldly to the fly. These shoals are likely to be fairly mobile and the angler will need to be light on his feet to keep in touch with them.

Fly selection   A Marabou Viva is an exceptionally good early season fly for searching mid water levels and deeper (sizes 8/10). My Standard Nymph will also produce very good results when the fish are detected on or near the surface (size 10).

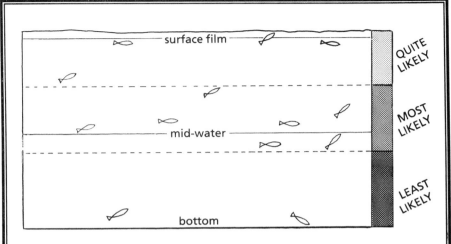

Fish Depth Guide – April

Retrieve   When fishing the Viva deep, a slow figure of eight or a gentle pull and pause routine should do the trick. But if the trout are located higher in the water (mid to upper levels) this usually suggests they're likely to be more active. As a consequence the speed of these two retrieve patterns should be increased slightly. The Standard Nymph is best fished with a brisk figure of eight retrieve.

Conditions on the day   Weather conditions on the day can affect the depth at which the trout patrol and subsequently the style of your retrieve. A dull April day is almost always cold and discourages surface activity, whereas some warming sunshine can have the opposite effect, stimulating the fish into investigating the upper water layers. As ever a little surface ripple should be welcomed but heavy wind this early in the season is bad news, serving only to delay the general warming process.

❧ MAY ❧

GENERAL ADVICE

The difference between April and May is always likely to be fairly dramatic for the angler and I'm not just talking about the weather. Temperatures will be rising steadily by now and the longer days are already with us. Spring proper has arrived and, with the best of the season still to come, who could blame us for feeling optimistic? But there is a perverse side to this month that we need to be aware of if we are to make the most of the next few weeks.

Probably the single most important event to fish and fishermen alike will be the explosion of insect life brought about by the increase in water temperature mentioned earlier. Prolific insect life offers the fish a ready source of protein, enabling them to put on weight and improve their physical condition. Widespread hatches of fly also benefit the angler by splitting up those tight shoals of stockies we talked about last month, and that must be a good thing. However, this sudden increase in natural food brings about a subtle change in the fish's behaviour and if anglers didn't realize it already they're soon made aware that heavy fly hatches don't always mean easy fishing. In fact, very often the exact opposite is true. The more natural food is available to the fish the more selective they can afford to become when feeding and you may well find the trout far less inclined to chase a badly fished fly in May than they were in April when insect life was scarce.

As a general rule the absence of fly should encourage the use of attractor patterns which, as their title suggests, might just attract the attention of fish when there is little or no natural food about. (I class lures as attractor flies.) By the same token, the heavier the hatch the more the angler should consider fishing a natural imitation.

In order that you understand fully what I am saying let me ask you to put yourself in the position of the fish for a moment. Just imagine that you're cruising comfortably in the warm surface water, feeding sedately on hatching olive nymphs. There's no need to hurry, there's plenty for all. Then, flashing past the end of your nose goes a fluorescent orange lure, the angler stripping it back as fast as he can go. Now, here's the question: will you leave the nymphs you've been feeding on and pursue it? Probably not. You're not *that* hungry. But half a minute later a damsel nymph wriggles slowly into view just a foot or two away. Are you going to ignore it? Not likely. You'll flick your tail, slide over there and snap it up, counting it as a bonus! Do you see what I mean?

Finding the Fish

If I was asked to highlight one of the major differences between the average angler and the true expert I think I'd plump for the latter's ability to locate the fish. Some people it seems have an in-bred knack of knowing where the fish are likely to be. I once had a friend who was a perfect example of such a man. Often, on dour days, we'd walk the bank together searching for some sign. Then, for no apparent reason, he'd stop and peer out across the water like a gun dog who'd spotted game. Hard as I tried I couldn't work out what it was that caused him to sense the proximity of fish but his laconic 'I'll just give it a go here' was usually followed soon after by the splashing of an angry trout trying to dodge the net.

I don't believe there is anything particularly mysterious about these characters. They're simply more sensitive to what is going on around them than the rest of us. They read the signs, often quite unconsciously, and the signs register, producing what anglers refer to as a 'gut feel'. But the signs are there for us all to see if we care to look. It's just a matter of learning to recognize them. (See Reading the Signs on page 23.)

Tactics

Once the fish have been found you should base your tactics upon two things: the fish's behaviour and the evidence of hatching fly. If the fish are surging and splashing vigorously then by all means try your favourite lure. But, if as often happens at this time of year, the rise has been brought about by a hatch of fly, then the fish are likely to be feeding upon the insect and you should be thinking of offering them something similar. The species we should expect to see this month will be mainly buzzers and olives with an outside chance of damsel nymphs if the weather has been particularly warm.

It is not normally necessary to match the hatching insect exactly unless the hatch is very dense. For example, if a few pond olives begin to show it is not absolutely vital that you fish with an Olive Nymph. A Pheasant Tail or Hare's Ear could do just as well. However, the more the hatch develops the harder you'll have to work matching the hatching insect. One tip worth remembering: if the hatch does become very dense and offers are hard to generate even though you're fishing the right pattern, try stepping up to a larger size, say from a size 12 to a 10. The thinking behind this strategy is simply that we need to be assured that our flies will be seen by the fish in amongst the thousands of other hatching insects.

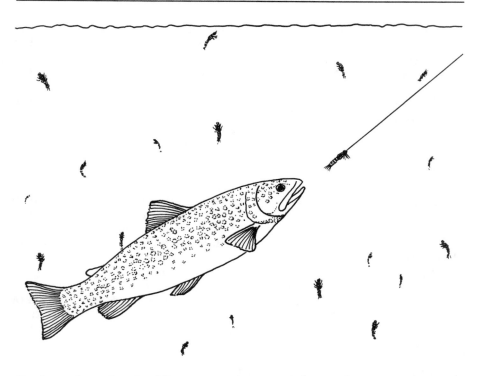

During a dense hatch of fly, try stepping up to a larger size to ensure your artificial is seen by the fish amongst the thousands of other hatching insects.

Practice

Alright then, that's enough preaching for a while. Let's now have an imaginary day's fishing at your local water so that we can put into practice some of the points we've talked about.

It's not a bad day for May, a bit on the bright side but thankfully not that harsh brightness of high summer that can make fishing so difficult. There has been no sign of rising fish at all during the morning but you're not too unhappy. The fish bag in your hand feels pleasantly heavy, thanks to the two rainbows that came to the Viva earlier on. You spent the morning exploring the margins, fishing your fly slow and deep. The trout probably took it for a cased caddis. The only disappointment so far has been the fish that came unstuck shortly after hooking. It felt a little better than the average stockie.

It's twenty minutes after lunch before you see the first rise of the day: two fish just fifty yards further along the bank, and you quicken your pace in case someone else has spotted them too. By the time you're in position several fish have started to 'bulge' under the surface well within casting range. They're nymphing trout, you're certain of that, but what fly are they taking? At that moment you see the first olive dun flutter skywards.

You try them first with the Viva, twitching it seductively through the shoal, but apart from the briefest pluck on the first cast, they won't have it. You switch to a floating line with a size 12 Olive Nymph on the point. After the next cast the fly is allowed to sink twelve inches before you begin your retrieve and the offer that follows is unmissable, the line drawing away from you in the classic nymph take.

Just half a minute later you slip your third rainbow into the bag, not a big fish but very welcome. Two more follow soon after and you are beginning to enjoy yourself when, quite suddenly, the hatch increases in volume and despite frenzied fish activity you are finding offers hard to generate. You change to a hatching olive pattern, still a size 12, but although the water is now alive with fish the only offers you're getting are short sharp taps that are probably line bites. Frustrated and slightly desperate you fish on, the speed of your retrieve increasing all the time.

Alright, that's enough! It's time to stop for a moment and gather your wits rather than continuing to thrash the water thoughtlessly. Just take a couple of steps back and pour yourself a coffee before you try one of those bigger Olive Nymphs you tied for exactly this sort of situation. Yes, I know it's quite a bit bigger than the naturals coming off but give it a go anyway.

After draining your cup and making the necessary changes to the fly you cast it once more in amongst the fish. You straighten the line and before you can catch your breath everything tightens up, the rod tip pulls around and a fish is on. There you are, it *was* worth the effort. Another fish in the bag and a nice one too. Nearer three pounds than two!

Then, almost as quickly as it started, the action begins to diminish and you sense that the peak has passed. Only the odd fish is showing now but it's still worth one last change in tactics. Off comes the large Olive Nymph and on goes a heavily leaded version of the same thing. You toss it with a plop into the water, roughly where the fish were rising five minutes earlier. After tidying the line you leave the fly to sink, watching like a hawk for the offer that might come 'on the drop'. Nothing. It sinks to five feet with no indication of a take and so you begin your retrieve, nipping the fly back in a gentle figure of eight. Still nothing. Ah well, it was worth a try. Then, with the fly almost at the end of the retrieve, a solitary fish rises in front of you. You lift the rod quickly, trying to throw the line behind you for one last cast. At that precise moment the fish that had followed the fly from the moment it entered the water makes up its mind to take it. There is a savage snatch, a boiling rise and the fish is gone, taking the fly and two feet of leader with it!

There are few worse feelings than losing a fish but knowing that it will happen again and again tends to make the angler philosophical – when he's stopped cursing that is! 'Always fish the cast out' – one of the basic rules of angling. Remember? Still you fished well enough to

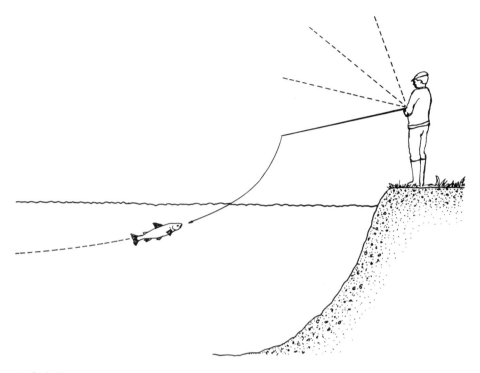

Fish follows fly and grabs hold as angler is lifting off to re-cast.

deceive the trout and that's what counts. There are six fish in your bag
that could have been eight with any luck. You caught them because you
were prepared to adopt a flexible approach to your fishing which is the
secret of success at any time of the year.

Reading the Signs

The simplest and most obvious indication that there are fish in the
vicinity is when they actually show themselves on the surface. In the
case of rainbow trout they regularly display quite boldly, rolling
splashily and sometimes leaping several feet clear of the water. Surface
activity is, however, not always so obvious and it takes a sharp pair of
eyes and plenty of practice to spot that tell-tale 'bulging' of the surface
film caused by a trout moving quickly to intercept an ascending nymph.

 If there is no surface activity you could do a lot worse than to search
for evidence of hatching flies. Birds can be a great help at times like this,
particularly the swallows and martins. When you see them wheeling
and swooping close to the surface they're not exercising, they've found
flies. You can bank on it! As a general rule, if you can find a few insects

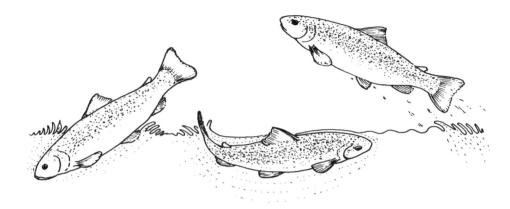

Rainbow trout displaying by leaping and rolling.

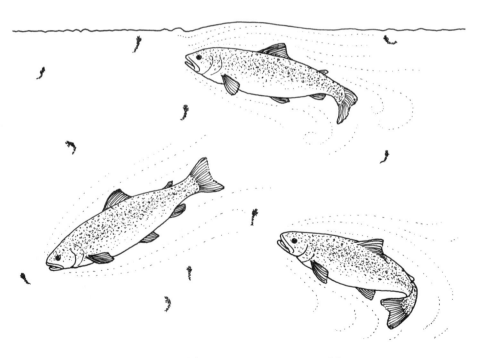

Bulging of the surface caused by a trout moving quickly to intercept an ascending nymph.

you'll have found a few fish too. They may not necessarily be feeding on the top. They could well be grubbing about on the bottom, or picking off nymphs in mid water as the insects struggle towards the surface in preparation for hatching.

Finding the depth at which fish are feeding is never the easiest of tasks for the angler but if we take a pace back and look logically at the problem perhaps it is not quite as difficult as we first thought. It is not unreasonable to suppose that the majority of fish will be found close to the bulk of the food source which means that, if the trout discover the insects early, let's say at the commencement of the hatch, they are likely to be on or near the bottom. But, as the volume of hatching flies increases, the fish will drift upwards with the main body of the hatch, giving themselves ample opportunity to make the most of what is on offer. Finally, when the hatch is at its peak, the fish will be found near the surface, mopping up insects as they struggle to break through the surface film and, for the unfortunate few who thought they'd escaped, sucking down flies from right off the top as they sit there drying newly opened wings.

Of all the various weather conditions that affect our sport none has more influence than the wind. On those days when hatching flies are scarce the bank into which the wind is blowing is usually the more

Swallows and martins swooping close to the surface indicate a hatch of fly.

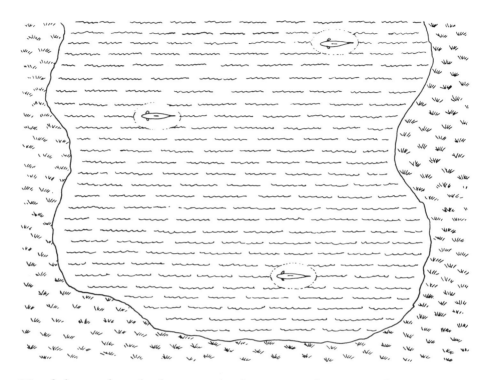

Watch for patches of calm appearing in amongst the waves. These are caused by rising fish displacing water.

productive. The trout will forage in this rough water, searching for morsels of food that the wind might have delivered. It is also worth noting that fish usually feed quite boldly in a good ripple and are far easier to tempt than in flat calm conditions. Spotting a rise in rough water is not as difficult as you might imagine once you know what to look for. Watch for sudden patches of calm appearing in amongst the waves. These are caused by rising fish displacing water.

Lastly, in the absence of all other signs, I'd suggest you concentrate your search in areas of shallow water and by that I mean water less than fifteen feet deep. Very few insects exist in the cold darkness of the deeper water and, of course, where the insects thrive you'll find the trout!

TWO FLIES FOR MAY

Predicting the weather is a science in which I claim no expertise. But, if April has been at all normal, I have no doubt that you will already have fished through a real mixed bag of conditions ranging from periods of bitter, bone-chilling cold with winds so heavy it's an effort just keeping the line in the air, to gentler, balmy days with the sun strong enough to warm your face and the breeze a mere zephyr, falsely proclaiming summer to be just around the corner.

However, despite Mother Nature's attempts to convince us otherwise, we know that it is not usually until May that the water begins to warm up significantly. This increase in temperature triggers an almost immediate response from the early aquatic insects which suddenly become much more active. That, quite simply, is the big difference between the two months and why my recommended flies for May are both 'natural' imitations.

The Bloodworm

A couple of years ago in May I paid a visit to the Packington Fishery, near Meriden in Warwickshire, which is not far from my home. By the time I arrived at the waterside most of the bank space on the two larger pools was occupied. I suppose I could have squeezed in somewhere but I hate fishing shoulder to shoulder and so headed for a quiet bay on the smallest pool, Burnet Iron. The bank at the top end of Burnet is very steep, making casting difficult (which is probably why no one was there that morning), but it's an area that often holds fish during the early part of the season. With the exception of two anglers in a boat nearby I had that end of the pool to myself which pleased me. They recognized me and we chatted as I tackled up. Apparently they'd been there since 6 a.m. and although offers had been plentiful only two fish had 'stuck' up to that time.

I began with my usual Standard Nymph pattern, size 12, fishing it hard on the bottom in five feet of water. The lake bed at that point is soft and silty and, most important, pretty well clear of weed. There followed twenty minutes of sheer frustration as every cast was greeted with an offer of some kind from the fish, most of them gentle little pulls that I simply couldn't connect with. It was due more to luck than skill when a small stockie finally hooked itself. I netted it quickly, intending to spoon it for clues, but found it wasn't necessary. That little rainbow was stuffed to the gills with bloodworms!

I didn't hang about, believe me. My other rod was loaded with a sinking line and a single fly, a Viva of course, and it took only moments to replace that tried and trusty friend with a Bloodworm pattern. The whole operation couldn't have taken any longer than two minutes, yet they would prove to be the most vital one hundred and twenty seconds of the day.

I re-cast and, even though the water was relatively shallow, waited a good thirty seconds before beginning my retrieve. I needed to be sure that everything, line, leader and fly, were safely down on the bottom. The usual thoughts went through my head as I counted silently to myself. 'Seventeen,' where's the landing net? 'Eighteen,' you're standing on it! 'Nineteen,' keep watching the line at the rod tip. 'Twenty,' here we go.

I'm not sure if I moved the fly at all before the fish took hold. If I did it was no more than inches. There was no dramatic snatch, no long pull, just solid resistance. I tightened up sedately and the fish was on. It was as simple as that. If someone considering taking up the sport had watched me during the next few minutes then catching trout on a fly would have seemed the easiest thing in the world! Seven casts, seven offers, five fish (two slipped the hook).

I stopped fishing at that point. It would have proved nothing to have gone on taking fish after fish. Perhaps years ago I might have done so, I'm ashamed to say, but nowadays solving the problem of *how* to catch has become more important to me than the act itself. And now perhaps you'd excuse me for one moment while I give myself a mental kick in the pants. I'm not here to preach fishing philosophy. We should be talking about the attractions of the humble bloodworm, the larval stage of the midge.

How to Fish It

Although fishing a Bloodworm pattern is essentially an uncomplicated business, it still requires a little detective work on our part. Having said that, only two factors need influence us in our choice of where to fish: a nice clean bottom, and some evidence of earlier buzzer activity. Let's take a moment to look at them individually.

1. The fly *must* be fished hard on the bottom, nowhere else will do, and so it's sunk line tactics. Any weed or other debris in the area will make that impossible. While I'm on the subject of lines let me mention the leader: keep it short and simple – ten feet of 4 lb breaking strain nylon is ideal.

2. Evidence of earlier buzzer activity is easy enough to recognize. Simply look for empty shucks at the water's edge. But be careful, you need also to note the strength and direction of the wind. Buzzer shucks can drift quite a long way in a short space of time. I should also like to mention the value of spooning any fish caught. There cannot be a less complicated way of discovering exactly what the fish are feeding on.

With regard to how you retrieve the fly, let me say this: it will almost always be too fast! Remember, it is the movement of a worm you're trying to imitate. I've found the best retrieve to be a very gentle pull of just a few inches, followed by a pause of five or six seconds. Your intention must be to keep the fly bumping along the bottom as slowly as possible. In my experience the fish usually picks up fly between pulls, which is why the bite registers as the line going 'heavy', but any resistance should be met with a firm strike.

This pattern is not one that will see the light of day every time you go fishing. It is, in all honesty, a bit of a 'special'. But at the right time and in the right place it can wreak terrible havoc to the trout stocks of any fishery and on that basis alone is worth its place in your fly box.

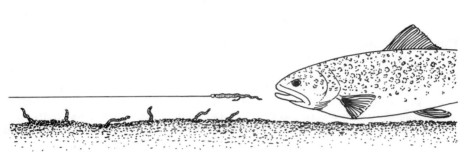

soft silty bottom

The fly must be fished as close to the bottom as possible when the fish are feeding on bloodworms. Nowhere else will do!

Tying Instructions

HOOK: Partridge Captain Hamilton H1A, size 12.
THREAD: Red.
BODY: Tying thread overwound with brown marabou.
RIB: Copper wire.
TAIL: Red marabou.
WING: Red/brown marabou mix.

Take the thread in neat, touching coils down the hook shank from eye to bend. At that point catch in your rib and tie a very sparse tail (no more than eight fibres), plus two brown fibres for overwinding the body. Then take the tying silk back along the hook shank in the direction of the eye, still keeping the coils neat and touching. Now comes the tricky part of the job. Take the two brown marabou fibres and wind them gently around the hook shank in nice open turns so that they overlay the red silk body but do not obscure it totally. You'll need a very delicate touch to do this properly. The slightest excess pressure will cause them to snap. Tie off these fibres and follow them with the wire rib. The rib is simply reinforcement against the ravages of a trout's teeth. Last, but not least, mix a little red and brown marabou to form the slimmest possible wing, and tie in. Finish off with a small, neatly whipped head.

The secret to tying this fly well is to keep all the materials to an absolute minimum. It is better to under-dress rather than over. If you want to test whether you've got it right tie the fly on a foot of nylon, soak it well in a bowl of water, then jig it up and down a few times. When you lift it out you'll know straightaway if you've been successful.

The Buzzer Nymph

There has probably been more written about this insignificant looking little fly than any other British pattern. I myself have contributed many thousands of words, singing its praises from the rooftops, and yet, recently, the Buzzer Nymph has fallen quite out of fashion. Why that should be I really don't know, though I suspect the popularity of large flies tied with modern fluorescent materials has much to do with it. Have we literally been blinded by them?

To truly understand the value of the Buzzer Nymph in fly fishing we need first to look briefly at the insect it is tied to represent. The midge family (the Chironomids) is vast and ubiquitous, existing in almost every pond, stream, river and lake the length and breadth of the country. Every year countless billions of these tiny flies hatch, it seems, with the sole purpose of making life a misery for all other living creatures. (Ever tried picnicking on the shores of a Scottish loch in summer?)

The number of insects involved in a really dense hatch of midges (anglers call them buzzers because of the noise made by their wings) is quite staggering. Millions, literally millions of them can hatch in a single brief evening period. But what I find even more astounding is that for every one insect that escapes from the surface of the water, many,

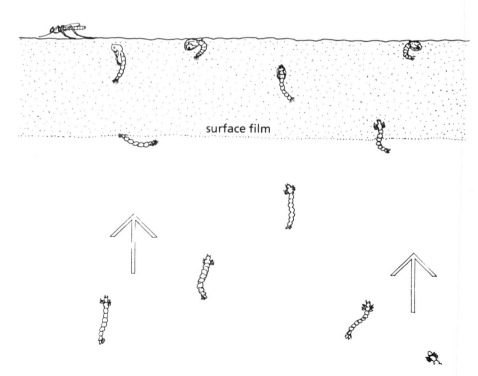

surface film

Hatching buzzer nymphs trapped in the surface film.

many more are eaten by the fish as they make the perilous ascent from the bed of their watery home in preparation for hatching.

It is during this nymphal or intermediate stage, between larva (bloodworm) and the adult fly, that the insect is at its most vulnerable. It makes sense therefore that we anglers should have a pattern that represents this stage of development. Hence the Buzzer Nymph.

When pupation takes place and the bloodworm is transformed into this free swimming creature, its only defence against the trout is in the vastness of its numbers. All fish will eat buzzer nymphs but none more enthusiastically than the trout. It is one of the few insects that can preoccupy them totally. This is especially true when the mass migration to the surface occurs prior to a hatch taking place. The fish rise in the water with the main body of insects, picking the nymphs off as they ascend, but it is when the majority of hatching flies are trapped in the surface film that the real feast begins. The density of the water in the surface film is much greater than elsewhere and it takes these tiny, frail creatures some time to break through. The trout can now afford to take their time. They simply cruise along, mouths open, oblivious to everything else but what is in front of them. Can you see now the importance of a proper artificial for times like this?

How to Fish It

For me the great attraction in buzzer fishing is that it is essentially a visual experience with floating lines and surface feeding trout. Certainly it is possible to catch fish with Buzzer Nymphs on a sinking line, fishing deep, but, for me at least, there is considerably less enjoyment to be had from using such tactics. I much prefer a line that floats and two or three flies on the cast, all Buzzers, all of differing colours. Colour identification can be a problem for the angler. If the flies hatching are green, or black, or orange, it is a waste of time offering the fish some other hue. They're unlikely to accept it. However, with three flies on the cast you're three times more likely to strike lucky. I usually plump for black on the point, green on the first dropper and brown or orange on the second. Once I have a fish on the bank my marrow spoon will soon reveal the exact colour of the hatching insects.

Taking any fish from the surface requires a rather more delicate approach than if we were fishing deep. This is particularly true of Buzzer

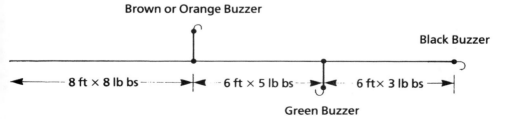

Preferred leader set-up for buzzer fishing.

fishing. I would suggest a leader of at least eighteen feet, twenty if you can manage it, graduated down to a point of no more than 4 lb breaking strain. My personal choice is for a leader made up of three lengths of nylon, eight feet of 8 lb breaking strain, followed by six feet of 5 lb, and finally six feet of 3 lb. That's twenty feet overall.

Before beginning to fish I diligently de-grease all three sections of my leader using a mixture of Fuller's earth, washing-up liquid and a little water. This gives a nice smooth paste that quickly strips grease from the line, allowing it to sink just sub-surface under its own weight. The importance of getting the line down into the surface film should not be under estimated, particularly in flat calm conditions. Floating nylon is horribly visible and creates enough of a disturbance on the retrieve to spook any fish.

Once the fish have been found and you have established that they are indeed feeding on buzzers, begin fishing by concentrating on one fish only. Do your best to judge the direction in which it is travelling and put your flies out well before it gets there. That gives you time to straighten the line and tidy things up generally. Then, when you're sure the fish is close to where your cast landed, simply lift the rod tip a few inches. This causes your flies, that by now will have sunk a few inches into the surface film, to suddenly wriggle upwards in a most lifelike manner.

If you've got it right there will be no violent snatch, just a gentle boil in the water and a twitch on the line. Well done! The fish has taken the fly. Now please don't go and spoil all your good work with a great, wrenching strike. Remember that fine tippet you're using. Simply lift the rod and let the fish do the rest.

If you are fortunate enough to come across a truly heavy hatch of buzzers, when it seems every fish in the pool is on the surface, don't bother with trying to identify the feeding route of individuals. Just put your flies where there is plenty of activity and retrieve them with gentle six inch pulls.

Tying Instructions

HOOK: Partridge GRS 2A, size 16/14/12/10.
THREAD: Main colours are black, green, red, brown and orange.
BODY: Tying thread.
RIB: Gold/silver wire.
THORAX: Seal's fur or substitute.
BREATHING FILAMENTS: White body wool.
WING CASE: Pheasant tail.

Take a few wisps of white body wool, approximately twice the length of the hook, and position them along the shank so that they overlap evenly at both ends. Then, beginning at the eye of the hook, tie these in position. At the same time, form the body of the fly, working down towards the hook bend in neat, touching turns. It is important that when you reach the bend of the hook you continue a little way around

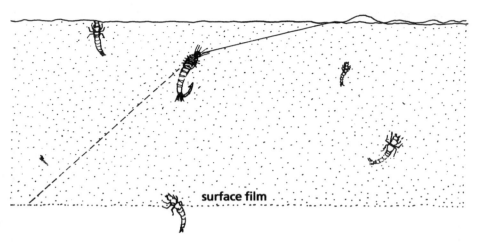

A gentle lift of the rod tip causes the fly to wriggle upward in a most realistic fashion.

it, giving the body that distinctive hook shape. Now catch in the wire rib before taking the thread back towards the eye, overwinding the first layer of thread with a second. When you have covered roughly two-thirds of the hook shank with the second layer you can stop and begin winding on the rib. Tie this in securely and, while you're at it, fix a small slip of pheasant tail feather by its tip. The rest is very straightforward. Dub on a sparse thorax then fold the pheasant tail slip up and over in the wing case position. That's it, all done! Oh, I almost forgot – take a pair of sharp scissors and trim off the excess white body wool at the head and tail of the fly. The breathing filaments should be understated rather than too obvious.

THINGS TO REMEMBER
᧤ MAY ᧥

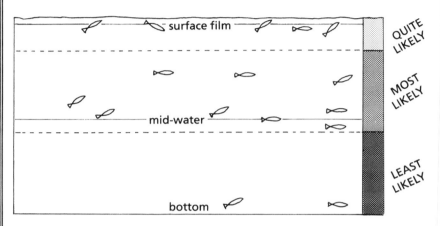

Fish Depth Guide – May

Water temperature Beginning to rise. Even something as unscientific as a finger in the water can prove how quickly the surface layers are warming.

Fly hatches We can expect regular hatches of fly this month with buzzers to the fore. Light hatching activity during the day will often build to a crescendo as dusk approaches. The Ephemeroptera family will also be putting in an appearance, although the heavier hatches of this species tend to take place later in the month, continuing into June.

Fish behaviour With an increasing supply of natural food now available the trout can afford to behave slightly more circumspectly and are less likely to chase after badly fished flies. Surface feeding activity should be on the increase.

Fly selection The use of imitative patterns should be uppermost in the angler's mind, matching the hatching insect where possible. A Bloodworm pattern (size 12) fished on the bottom will often produce good results during the daylight hours, with the Buzzer Nymph (sizes 16 to 10) coming into its own as and when surface feeding begins. An Olive Nymph (size 12) is also a useful general pattern for May.

Retrieve   For the Bloodworm pattern I would suggest a *very* gentle pull and pause routine. A similar, but slightly quicker, retrieve pattern can be used for fishing the Buzzers on or near the surface, with a slow figure of eight as an alternative. The Olive Nymph is usually best fished figure of eight style.

Conditions on the day   May sunshine is rarely harsh enough to drive the fish into deeper water and even on bright days there should still be plenty of surface activity. Any ripple or choppiness caused by the wind will be advantageous to anglers presenting flies on the surface.

JUNE

General Advice

I find it quite impossible to think of June without my mind conjuring up pictures of misty early mornings with the dew still clinging white to the grass and the flat, earthy smell of drying mud and fresh water, or of soft, hawthorn scented evenings and sitting quietly with friends at the water's edge, waiting expectantly for the first rise.

In case you hadn't guessed already June is my favourite month of the season and I can't imagine a lovelier time of year to be by the waterside. Certainly the odd, unseasonably cold day will still plague us but we need to look no further than the bank-side vegetation, bursting with fresh greenery, to be reminded that summer really has arrived.

June tends, on the whole, to be a bright dry month. The days are now at their longest and it is possible, if you have the stamina, to fish solidly for up to sixteen hours a day, though I wouldn't recommend it. I regard June more as a dish of fine fruits from which we anglers can take our pick, rather than a plate of grey porridge on which to gorge ourselves. But if you have no choice other than fishing between the hours of 9 a.m. and 6 p.m. then I'd suggest you choose a day when some cloud cover is forecast. Sport can be first class for quite long periods under overcast skies, but bright hot days should be avoided if at all possible for these conditions usually mean hard fishing – though a good stiff breeze and a vigorous ripple can often save the day. However, if you intend to make the most of your time from now through to September, it is early mornings and late evenings that are the magical times for the angler. I find it almost sinfully pleasurable arriving fresh at my local fishery an hour before sunset with my appetite sharpened by the knowledge that the best of the fishing is still to come.

So far this season only two species of fly have been of any real significance to anglers, the upwinged flies or, as they are more commonly known, olives (Ephemeroptera), and of course the buzzers (Chironomid). These will both continue to be of value during June but the time has now come to add two more very important flies to our list, one of which always hatches in daylight while the other prefers to emerge after sunset. I'm talking about the damsel fly and the family of sedge flies.

Damsel Flies

Let's begin by looking in some detail at the damsels. Although this particular insect does not hatch in vast numbers like the buzzers, I still regard it as being one of the most important of all the aquatic flies to the bank angler. In order for you to understand why I should hold this creature in such high esteem it is necessary for me to spend a few moments describing its hatching behaviour.

If ever nature set out to create a 'meals on wheels' service for the trout I think it would look and behave a lot like the damsel nymph. Hatching takes place on dry land and always occurs during daylight hours, the nymphs ascending to the surface often well away from the nearest stretch of bank, leaving themselves a long and perilous journey across the top. They're not helped by a vigorous, eel-like swimming action that can create quite a commotion. It's almost as if they were crying out to be eaten. Remember, these are large insects and I've

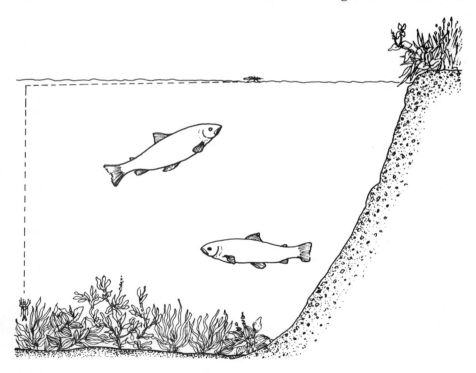

Damsel nymphs ascend to the surface often well away from the nearest bank, leaving themselves a long and perilous journey.

actually seen them, in calm conditions, leaving a tiny wake behind them in their mad dash towards dry land. Needless to say a large percentage of them never make it. Those that do climb clear of the water, sometimes onto bank-side vegetation and sometimes onto dry land proper, where the final transformation to the adult fly takes place. I would like to stress at this point that it is only in its nymphal state that this fly is of use to the angler. I have no doubt that the trout would take an adult fly if it were given the opportunity, but when was the last time you saw a damsel – or dragonfly for that matter – settle directly onto the surface of the water? On bank-side vegetation, yes, even on your rod tip if you sit still long enough, but on the water? I hesitate to use the word 'never', so let's just say that it's a rare occurrence!

Tactics

To fish a damsel nymph requires a certain amount of faith for it's not as if you're likely to see millions of these creatures hatching and know that the time is right for fishing the artificial. So, let me offer you some assurances. From late May, and on through the rest of the summer, damsel nymphs will be heading shorewards in preparation for hatching and, more importantly, the trout will be on the lookout for them. When are the best times to fish this fly? I'm tempted to say 'anytime' but ideally it will be the kind of day when there are hatching flies on the water but not enough to provoke a proper rise and the fish are showing only spasmodically. In other words, normal summer conditions. It's at times like this that the damsel will pay its way.

This is an artificial that should always be fished on or near the surface. I work on the principle that the higher in the water it is fished the more effective it becomes which is why, when tying this pattern, I prefer mine unleaded. I'm not suggesting that when fished deep on a sinking line it will not take a few trout, it's just that if I feel the time is right for using deep-sunk nymph tactics I have other patterns that would be better suited.

Speed of retrieve is inevitably difficult to translate from paper to practice and so, in order to avoid confusion, I'll simply say that like all nymph patterns the damsel is best fished slowly and continuously and that I find a gentle figure of eight retrieve perfect for the job.

Before I finish with this fly I'd like to offer a word of warning. Fishing a damsel up in the surface film can provoke truly savage 'takes' and I would recommend a point of at least 5 lb breaking strain in order to avoid the embarrassment of being broken by a fish taking at speed. It seems that when the trout decide to dine upon damsels they do so with gusto!

Sedge Flies

Whether or not we see a proper hatch of sedges in June depends very much upon the weather or, to be more precise, the temperature. In the colder parts of the country a regular hatch is unlikely but the further south you go the better your chances become. So, if this species of insect is unlikely to put in much of an appearance then why bother to mention it at all? Good question, and the answer is quite simple. If June turns out to be a real 'scorcher', and you're prepared to stay on late at your local fishery, then there's every chance that you'll witness a sedge hatch before the month is out. And unless you are prepared with a few good imitations in your fly box you could miss out on the opportunity of a lifetime for there are very few insects that provoke a rise quite like the sedge. So, treat this paragraph as a reminder, a gentle nudge in the ribs. I'll go into further detail on this topic in the next chapter.

Hard Times

No matter how well you plan your fishing there is always the possibility that you will find yourself having to fish through the middle hours of a day more suited to sun bathing than angling. You must know the sort of day I mean, when the sun blazes down from a sky so blue it might have come straight from a child's paintbox and there's not a breath of wind to ripple the surface of the water. Only the coots show any signs of life as they fidget around the margins. Yes, I know we'd be better off at home stretched out in a deckchair on the lawn, but we're here now, at the fishery, and so what can we do – apart from hoping for some kind of miracle?

Hot, flat conditions are hard on all anglers but it is the committed bank fisherman who suffers most. The hot sun blazing down not only warms up the surface layers of water, it also lowers the oxygen content, forcing the fish to seek the cooler, deeper areas that are often out of the bank angler's reach. It is possible to catch trout under these circumstances but we should be under no illusion, it will be desperately hard and the only crumb of comfort I can offer is that three fish caught on a day like this are worth nine or ten taken under normal conditions.

The time has now come to put away our floating lines and natural imitations. Sinking lines and lures are the order of the day. The trout we are hoping to catch will not be feeding in the true sense of the word and are unlikely to leave their station in the deeper water to chase a fly fished some distance above their heads. If we are to provoke a response it will be necessary to keep the fly in the immediate vicinity of the fish for as long as possible and hope to tease him into snapping at it.

Normally weighted lures would be useless for this purpose as they would be buried deep in a jungle of weed before the retrieve was half completed. No, this situation requires a set-up that is rather more specialized such as a fast sinking line and a buoyant Booby Nymph, perfect tools for the job in hand. Once the correct length of leader has been established (just long enough to allow the fly to float clear of the bottom weed) these Booby patterns can be fished as slow as you like. In fact I've actually witnessed anglers who, after casting, tied their lines to some immovable object on the bank and started lunch, their rods left unattended, and while they were tucking into coffee and sandwiches their lines have straightened with a 'clunk' as the fish hooked itself!

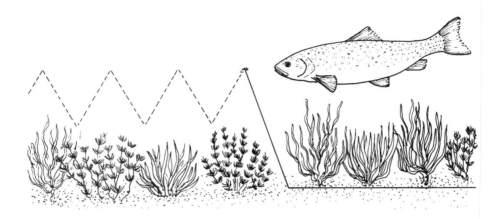

Once the correct length of leader has been established (just long enough to allow the fly to float clear of bottom weed), these Booby patterns can be fished as slow as you like.

Now this is most certainly not fly fishing and I'm not suggesting for one moment that anyone should try it. I'm simply using it as an example to show that it is not always necessary to retrieve the fly.

Tactics

The angler's first task must be to find the deeper water, and at times like this local knowledge is invaluable. However, if you find yourself at a strange fishery then a useful tip is to concentrate your efforts in areas where the bank falls steeply into the water for these are almost always the deepest spots. Gradual banks mean shallow water more often than not.

The problem of locating the fish often means adopting a rather mechanical approach to the search but if we can find twenty feet of water close in then we're in with a chance. Try to establish where the deeper stretch begins and start there, casting straight out in front of you. Give the line plenty of time to hit bottom before beginning a *very* slow pull and pause retrieve, certainly no quicker than one pull every seven or eight seconds. When the retrieve is completed move five yards further along the bank and repeat the procedure until you locate fish or run out of deep water. If you are fortunate enough to generate an offer my advice would be to move no further. Stick it out there for at least thirty minutes. You may have found a shoal and even if you have to wait some time for your next offer that's better than nothing at all.

The odd thing about this kind of dead slow retrieve is that, more often than not, the fish takes the fly when it is at rest, on the pause rather than the pull if you see what I mean. I had absolutely no idea why

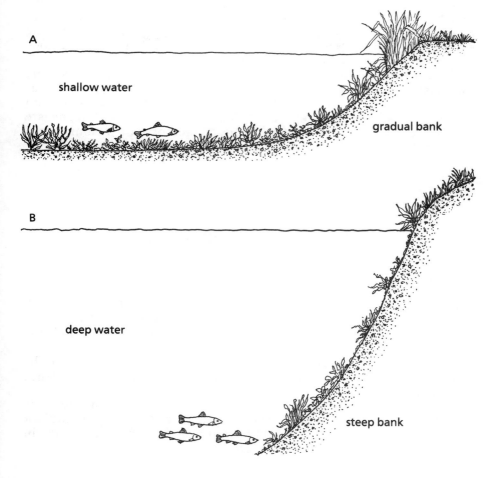

A

shallow water

gradual bank

B

deep water

steep bank

Gradual banks usually indicate shallow water (A), steep banks deep water (B).

that should be until last summer. I happened to be in the garden, taking a break after mowing the lawn. From the sanctuary of a bench under the lilac trees I watched the family cat, who is hardly more than a kitten, chasing a heavily laden bee through a flower bed. After several rather amateurish attempts she managed to knock it to the ground. She then took it into her mouth and gave it a bit of a 'chewing over' before spitting it out again. The bee, still alive though rather damp, began crawling away. The cat lay relaxed on the grass, watching. While the insect kept moving she was content just to watch but if it stopped she became agitated until, unable to bear the lack of movement any longer, she'd give it a clout with her paw to get it started again.

Now I may be wrong but I sense that something similar happens with this deep sunk retrieve and the Booby Nymphs. The fish watches the fly move, then pause, then move, then pause again, and, if the pause is long enough, the fish is aggravated into attacking the fly perhaps in the hope of driving it out of the immediate vicinity.

To be successful under these 'high summer' conditions requires more than just stamina. An angler needs concentration and self-discipline as well as an ounce or two of luck. And more often than not the reward will not reflect the effort expended. Few people if any will appreciate how well you may have fished for those three or four medium sized stockies. Still, hasn't that always been the angler's lot?

Two Flies for June

The Damsel Nymph

I believe that there are three good reasons for fishing a Damsel Nymph in preference to many other patterns during the next few weeks.

First, the fish will be expecting to see this fly on the move and that must be a good thing.

Secondly, we know that hatching takes place right throughout the daylight hours and, consequently, can fish the artificial with confidence from dawn to dusk.

And lastly, trout simply love eating damsel nymphs! They're a big insect when compared to most other aquatic species, a real mouthful for the fish and, like any other of God's creatures, the trout likes to take in as much protein as possible in one bite!

How to Fish It

Having already gone into some depth on how this fly should be fished I don't intend boring you with a lot of repetition. I would, however like to spend just a few moments talking about the leader. As always for surface fishing, it should be as long as you can manage, the longer the better. It should also be properly de-greased. I cannot stress highly enough the importance of this when fishing Nymphs and other natural imitations. Any disturbance created by the angler's retrieve must be kept to an absolute minimum.

With regard to how many flies you should fish on your cast, I would advise only one! It may be tempting to add a couple of other smaller patterns on the droppers, but you'd be far better off striving for a little extra distance when casting. Droppers then can become a nuisance unless your timing is spot on.

Tying Instructions

HOOK: Partridge Grey Shadow GRS2A, size 10.
THREAD: Olive green.
BODY: Olive ostrich herl.
THORAX: Olive seal's fur or substitute.
TAIL: Olive marabou.
HACKLE: Light green hen.
WING CASE: Pheasant tail.
RIB: Medium gold.

Put down the usual bed of tying silk from eye to bend, catching in the rib as you go. Then tie in a plump marabou tail that overhangs the hook bend by approximately three-quarters of an inch. If you're not sure exactly how much marabou is required for this why not take a pinch of feather in your fingers and wet it thoroughly. That should soon tell you how much is enough. Now tie in two strands of ostrich herl before taking the thread back towards the eye of the hook. Follow the thread with the ostrich herl, building up a short body that occupies two thirds of the hook shank, then wind on the rib. On a body as short as this you'll only manage three or four turns. Now for the wing case. Catch in the pheasant tail slip in the usual manner, then dub on a sparse thorax. It's important at this stage not to overdress the fly. A damsel nymph is a narrow gutted creature, not dissimilar to an earwig in profile. A bulky thorax would be altogether out of place. Besides, you need to leave room for a couple of turns of hackle yet. If you've followed my instructions to the letter you should have ample space to do that, and of course to tie in the wing case. Finish off with a nice, large head and there you have it. A Damsel Nymph à la Musgrove.

The Booby Nymph

Let me say right from the outset that the Booby Nymph is not my favourite pattern. Its effectiveness as a fish killer, however, cannot be disputed. The logic behind the combination of a fast sinking line and an ultra buoyant fly is really very simple. But there are a couple of things we anglers need to understand if we are to get the best out of this method.

To begin with, it is vital that the line sinks quickly and evenly. (You'd be surprised at how many don't.) We need to be confident that before we start the retrieve the full length of line we have cast is hard on the bottom. And secondly, but just as important, the fly we're using, whether shop-bought or home-made, should not simply float. It should float like a cork! It should be so buoyant that if held under water and then released it will shoot straight to the surface.

How to Fish It

Once again, having already gone into some detail on this subject in my general advice for June, I will not bore you with more of the same.

Having said that, there are still one or two points I feel duty bound to touch upon again in order to be sure you understand the practicalities of fishing this particular pattern.

Let's look once more, very briefly, at the leader set up. Try not to be too dogmatic about the length. For example, it is no earthly use fishing a leader of only twelve inches if the area into which you are casting has three feet of weed on the bottom. By the same token, ten feet of nylon over a bottom that is virtually clear of weed will not give you the desired effect either. Do you see what I mean? There are no hard and fast rules concerning Booby fishing. The only advice I can offer is that, if you really are concentrating on deep water areas, it is unlikely you'll need a leader much longer than three feet for, as we all know, you don't get prolific weed growth at great depth.

Once you have made the decision as to where you're going to concentrate your efforts, then it is important that you fish systematically. Let me give you an example. If your chosen area is a deep trench then begin at one end, casting straight out in front of you. If there is no response from the trout then start fan casting either side. If there is still no response then move ten yards along the bank and repeat the exercise. If you continue in this fashion until you run out of deep water you can be pretty sure of covering any fish in the vicinity. Sounds

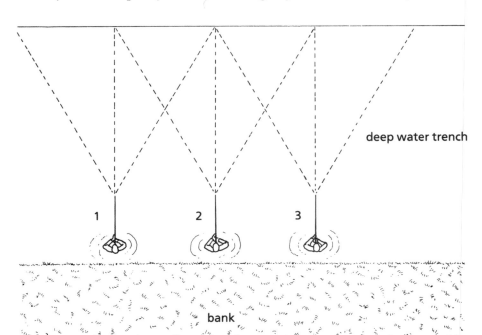

Angler casting over deep water (fan casting).

pretty straightforward doesn't it? There is, however, one more important point we should not overlook. It is absolutely vital that you allow enough time for the line to settle hard on the bottom. It's worth keeping in mind that no matter how long the fly is out there it is not going to snag up, so there's no need to rush things. Take your time.

Tying Instructions

HOOK: Partridge Streamer D3ST, size 10/12.
THREAD: Colour chosen to match that of the fly.
TAIL AND BODY: Marabou feather. (Any primary colour – I stick to black, white and orange.)
RIB: Flat silver tinsel.
EYES: Shaped plastazote with Lureflash optic-eyes added.

Lay down a neat bed of tying thread from the eye to the bend of the hook and catch in the rib. Then tie in a sparse tuft of marabou feather, the tips overhanging the hook bend by about three-quarters of an inch. Return the thread to a point two-thirds of the way back along the hook shank and leave it there for the time being. Simply attach a pair of hackle pliers (or a clothes peg) and leave it hanging. Now take the butt section of the marabou feather and use it to form a thin, fluffy body, winding it back towards the eye. Follow this with the rib and tie off.

That was the easy part – now for the tricky bit. Using a sharp knife cut out a narrow, oblong block of plastazote, three-quarters of an inch long by one-quarter square. Then, with scissors, nibble away at its centre until you have a rough hour glass shape. When you're happy with this, fix it on top of and at right angles to the hook shank, using a figure of eight tying, leaving just enough room for a neatly whipped head and a dab of superglue or varnish. The job of shaping the eyes should be left until the whipping has hardened off. Then it's simply a case of a neat hand, a little patience and a pair of sharp scissors. (The optic-eyes shown on my pattern aren't really necessary, but they amuse me!)

THINGS TO REMEMBER
ᘓ JUNE ᗧ

Water temperature   Now at an ideal level for both fish and insects.

Fly hatches   Insect activity is now peaking for the year. In addition to the buzzer and mayfly families, damsel flies will also be hatching during the daytime, offering the trout yet another source of food.

Fish behaviour On overcast days the trout often patrol the surface layers for prolonged periods. But in the event of hot sunshine, serious feeding is usually confined to early mornings and late evenings.

Fly selection Natural imitations fished high in the water will continue to be successful. The Damsel Nymph (size 10) is an excellent daytime pattern and will probably account for more fish than any other fly of its kind over the next few weeks. But if you're unlucky enough to find yourself out on a real scorcher of a day then the Booby Nymph (sizes 10/12) may prove to be your saviour.

Retrieve For the Damsel Nymph there is no better retrieve than a steady figure of eight. This mimics the creature's natural movements as well as we can hope to. With regard to the Booby Nymph, a slow pull and pause routine is as good as anything, with a very slow figure of eight as an alternative.

Conditions on the day June begins the three months of high summer and is a significant change point in the angling calendar. There is no doubt that breezy, overcast conditions can provide brilliant sport for the fly fisher this month. But, having said that, prolonged periods of hot sunshine produce exactly the opposite effect, discouraging the trout from feeding during the daytime. A strong wind and vigorous ripple will sometimes help, but on bright days it makes sense to concentrate angling activity to the early and late hours of the day.

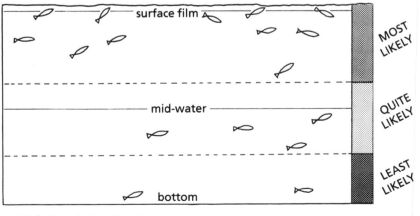

Fish Depth Guide – June

⁓ JULY ⁓

GENERAL ADVICE

Sedge Fishing

It had been a bright, hot, windless day and as usual I'd arrived at the pool far too early, but that period of relative inactivity, from 6 p.m. through till around 8 p.m., had become part and parcel of summer sedge fishing for me over the years. It was a time of delicious anticipation, an opportunity to chat with other anglers, to talk tactics and discuss last week's sport – who'd caught what and from where.

I resisted the temptation to begin right away, in fact it was almost an hour later when the need to wet a line got the better of me and I began throwing my flies into the flat mirror surface of the lake. It was a useless exercise, I knew that, but the desire to feel the rod flexing in my hand and to see the line sliding out over the water was just too great. Anyway, I might just pick up the odd 'idiot' fish, I told myself, and that would be a bonus before the serious business began.

The pool I was fishing had, like so many of our smaller waters, begun its life as a gravel pit. Time, clever fishery management and nature's forgiving hand had combined to produce from the original bare bones an extremely pretty, natural-looking water. It was, however, not a place I often frequented but word had reached me that some heavy hatches of sedge fly had taken place over the past few days and that thought alone had prompted me to pay a visit.

Eight o'clock arrived and the numbers on the bank began to thin. Tired anglers with red faces drifted away complaining towards the sanctuary of the clubhouse and the bar. It had been a desperately hard day, they all said, and I believed them. Even now, with the harsh light of broad day being softened by the onset of evening, the water still lay like a sheet of polished steel reflecting the fiery bulk of the setting sun. It was time to begin tackling up for the serious business still to come. I carried two rods, one loaded with a floating line, the other with a slow sinker. The second rod still sported the Appetizer that had kept me amused over the past hour. The fact that it managed to provoke one savage pull from a fish that unfortunately came unstuck owed more to this excellent fly's natural attraction than to my skill in fishing it. The Appetizer was changed for a Marabou Viva while on the other rod I mounted a Sedge Pupa as the point fly and an Invicta on the dropper. Both were size 10s.

After checking the knots for a second time I moved away from the busier stretches of bank, heading towards a quiet corner of the pool made up of three shallow bays of uniform depth, around eight feet. It was this general area, my friends had assured me, where a heavy sedge hatch had occurred two days earlier. Perched on top of a grassy mound where I could see almost the whole of the pool, I poured myself a coffee. The light was now failing fast and the surface of the water glowed like molten metal as the dying sun stretched itself in one last long reflection that reached out across the lake to paint the bullrushes at the base of my lookout post the colour of that most precious of all minerals. Sitting there with time to think the doubts came flooding in. What would I do if the sedge failed to show? Perhaps the hatch my friends witnessed two days earlier had been a one-off event. Angrily I pushed these negative thoughts to the back of my mind. Of course they'd show. And even if they didn't, something else was bound to hatch. I'd simply change tactics to suit the situation.

In this way I tried comforting myself, and failed! There had been no sign of hatching flies during the early part of the evening and as everyone knows both buzzers and olives usually give some warning of an impending hatch with the odd few insects putting in an early appearance. In the gathering gloom a match flared orange bright just thirty yards to my right, briefly illuminating the features of another angler who, like me, sat quietly near the water's edge. Seconds later the sharp smell of sulphur and burning tobacco reached my nostrils. I felt irritable, unreasonably so, at having to share that stretch of bank with someone else. I decided to move while there was still time.

Two minutes later, and fifty yards further along the bank, I saw the first rise. I hesitated, wondering for a moment if the disturbance had been caused by some water fowl I'd previously missed, but another rise seconds later set my pulses racing. They were trout and, even better, they were nymphing trout!

I stumbled further along the bank to where a short promontory jutted out a little way into the pool. In the few moments it took me to reach it, three more fish had risen and I saw the first sedge fly skitter across the surface, pale wings flapping clumsily as it tried to tear itself free from the water. Almost before it was airborne half a dozen others were hatching, right up in the surface film, and the trout began to rise regularly.

I took a few deep breaths to steady myself and put my second rod well out of the way. I didn't want to step on it while I was fishing. The landing net went close by my side where I could put a hand on it without looking. My first cast was a gentle one for the fish were no more than fifteen yards out. It was still light enough to see both the point fly and the Invicta dimple the surface as they fell. Straightening the line I waited a good six seconds before beginning the retrieve so that the Pupa would be fishing well sub-surface. The leader above the dropper had been lightly greased so I knew where the Invicta would be – right up in the surface film, where else?

Two feet into the retrieve the line went suddenly 'heavy' and I tightened up quite gently into my first fish, easing it out of the shoal and hoping that he'd cooperate by staying deep. Gentle pressure did the trick and half a minute later I netted a nice fat stockie with the minimum of fuss. It had taken the point fly. Two more followed in the next two casts, all coming to the Pupa. As I removed the hook from the second fish I noticed that sedge flies were beginning to cling to my clothes. I could even feel one or two in my hair. The hatch was becoming very dense indeed.

From that moment on every cast was greeted with an offer of some sort, though only twenty per cent resulted in fish on the bank as time after time they threw the hook. Close inspection of the flies revealed nothing. Both hooks were needle sharp. I should have changed them anyway but the light had almost gone. Fish were now crashing on the surface and I watched one pursue a fly as it attempted to take wing. The trout hit it like a small shark. Hands shaking with frustration I made another cast and, before I could begin my retrieve, the line sprang taut. This time the sensation was one of weight and strength but without the flashing speed we have come to associate with the rainbow. It took me half a minute to recognize the obvious. I'd hooked two fish at the same time! The only thing one can do under these circumstances is to allow the fish to fight against each other while you, the angler, apply steady pressure until they can be reached with the net. Fortunately for me the larger fish, a rainbow of around two pounds, had taken the dropper which meant it could be netted first. However, without help, I knew there was a good chance of losing the second. I was sliding the net under the first fish when an idea came into my mind. As I pulled the net towards me I laid down my rod and reached into my waistcoat pocket for the scissors that are always there. Without wasting a second I reached forward and snipped through the dropper. Lifting the net complete with fish and fly I deposited it on the bank behind me and grabbed hurriedly for my rod. I was in luck. The fish was still on and so exhausted that I was able to beach it quite easily.

Two more in the bag – that made seven. Only one more needed for my limit. It was now quite dark and a glance at my watch told me that only ten minutes remained before the beacon light on top of the lodge would begin to flash its warning message, calling all anglers to cease fishing. There was just time for one last effort. I found my second rod, unhooked the Viva from its holding ring near the butt and wet it thoroughly. It was now so dark that I couldn't see the rising fish properly. Not that it mattered. The water disturbance was easy enough to locate. Two false casts and out went the line. I began a fast retrieve as soon as the fly hit the water and the fish took it almost immediately, pulling the rod tip around savagely. For just a few precious, exhilarating seconds I felt the power of him as he ran hard to my left. Then, without warning, the rod recoiled and the line fell slack upon the water. Damn!

The best fish of the evening without a doubt and it had escaped. I stripped back quickly for another cast but before I could recover the line fully the beacon on the roof of the lodge began flashing its mournful message across the water. I looked at my watch. They were eight minutes early.

I was still too full of the excitement of the fishing to be thinking straight and for a moment I considered fishing on and challenging them later but, thankfully, common sense prevailed. It would have been a stupid and churlish way to end what had been a delightful evening, one that would be recalled with pleasure for some time in the future. Feeling just a little contrite I collected my tackle together and, with the fish bag weighing heavy in my hand, set off homeward through the darkness.

Those events just described took place almost three years ago. There have been many other occasions before and since when the sedge fly has provided me with good and exciting sport, yet none of them have stayed clear in my mind in the way this one did. The fates had conspired to present me with the 'classical' evening's sedge fishing, one where nature chose to obey all the rules. The weather, the insects, the fish, all behaved exactly as they should have done and it is for that reason I decided to use the occasion as the perfect example of what sedge fishing at its best can be like.

At this point I'd like to spend a few minutes analysing the separate ingredients that went into the making of that day so that we can really begin to understand their significance.

Weather Conditions

Although the day described had been hot and bright this in itself was not necessarily a contributing factor. To suggest that sedge flies will only hatch after a bright hot day would be nonsense. They will appear just as readily after a dull overcast day, *provided* that the evening is dry and fairly still – that is the vital ingredient. Wet and windy evenings are a washout in more ways than one.

The Insect

The fact that sedge flies belong to the order of *Trichoptera* is a matter of supreme indifference to most anglers and perhaps that is as it should be. Recognizing a sedge fly when we see it is quite sufficient for most people's needs. And so, for that purpose, let me say that the adult fly can best be described as resembling a moth. There are a great many sub-species within the overall family, some of which (the smaller darker varieties) are happy to hatch during the daylight hours. But from an angling viewpoint these daytime sedges are of little consequence for in my experience it is unusual for the trout to show much interest in them. Why that should be I simply don't know but one thing is certain, the same cannot be said for the larger, paler flies that begin to appear with the onset of night. A good hatch of these is almost guaranteed to produce a vigorous rise from the fish. But let me stress again, a sedge hatch of this kind is always an evening affair so if you're the kind of angler who likes to be in the pub by 7.30 then you're unlikely to ever witness such an event. I should also warn you that hatches can be very localized so it's important that you're in the right place at the right time. How to do that? I can only suggest you keep your ear to the ground. Anglers are notoriously poor at keeping secrets. If they know the location of regular sedge hatches someone is bound to spill the beans sooner or later.

The Event

Seeing trout react to the appearance of sedge flies is really quite something. It's what you might term a 'crash, bang, wallop' occasion! Water that only moments before seemed devoid of fish life is suddenly bulging as they begin feeding on the rising pupae. Then, as you watch, the first hatching flies appear. The surface dimples as those pupae lucky enough to have escaped the attentions of the trout break through. It takes only seconds for the pupal case to split and the adult fly to emerge. Then it's a quick stretch of cramped wings and a lumbering, rather clumsy attempt to take flight. A word often used to describe the sedge's efforts to get airborne is 'skittering' and it fits perfectly the flip-flopping, hip-hopping run-up this fly requires for take-off. Unfortunately this disturbance only serves to embolden the fish which come surging to the surface, mouths agape, pursuing the fly right up to the last second. It's exciting stuff, I don't mind telling you!

The Black Lure

The phenomenon of a black lure fished at the height of the hatch often producing the biggest fish is well known. Why this should happen I'm not sure, though I suspect it could be simple animal greed, the bigger fish seeing a fly that represents more of a mouthful. Anyway, the fact is that this tactic really works. Try it and see for yourself.

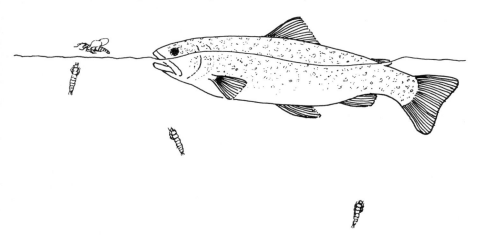

Fish come surging to the surface, mouths agape, pursuing the fly right up to the last second.

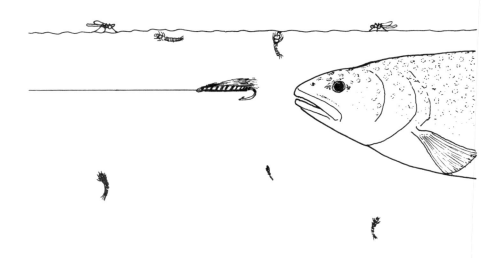

A black lure fished at the height of a sedge hatch often produces the biggest fish.

Tactics

So, what do we need to make the most of a situation like the one described earlier? Let's begin with the basics. You will need a floating line with a leader of around fifteen feet, graduated down to a tippet of 4 lb breaking strain. The Sedge Pupa should be mounted on the point and the Invicta on the dropper. By the way, if you've experienced problems in the past with droppers twisting around the leader, the odds are that they're too long. A three inch length is fine, two even better! The leader above the dropper should be lightly greased to keep the Invicta up near the surface while the Pupa is swimming a foot or so further down.

Once the hatch is under way I've rarely found it necessary to cast to individual rises. Just do your best to judge where the area of activity is greatest and put your flies into the middle of it. Once the cast is made give the Pupa a few seconds to drop below the surface film then begin your retrieve. Sedge pupae are good swimmers, especially when pursued by trout, so I prefer a quickish retrieve, smooth pulls of around twelve inches. The Invicta, which should be thoroughly wetted before use, should now be bulging the surface an inch or so down. You'll probably find most offers coming to the point fly which is hardly surprising when you realize just how vulnerable the pupa is at that stage. The Invicta is your banker. There are bound to be a number of feeding fish that become interested in those flies that are in the process of hatching and this traditional winged pattern is an excellent representation of the insect at that crucial stage. With its hackled yellow body and narrow folded wing it must look very attractive to the trout. The Invicta can also be used to catch those fish pursuing adult flies on the surface. It is, in all honesty, not as good as a proper floating sedge pattern but it will do at a push. Fished as the point fly on a greased line and twitched across the surface it will deceive the odd one or two for you.

When fishing a combination of flies we inevitably run the risk of hooking two fish at the same time. No matter what anyone else says I will never accept that this is at all clever or desirable. It is, quite simply, a nuisance! Not only is there a good chance of losing one of them, usually the biggest, complete with fly and nylon attached, there is also no real sense of fight from two trout who are effectively doing battle with each other. If it happens to you I can only advise that you apply steady pressure until the fish on the dropper can be reached. Net that one first and deal with the one on the point afterwards, if it's still on that is!

After reading the earlier paragraphs you may decide that sedge fishing is far too chancy a business for you. I hope not, but if you do I'll understand. You're absolutely right: there can be no guarantees. You may well take endless care in your preparation only to find that the insect fails to put in an appearance and you're left cursing the loss of a full day's fishing. You could judge conditions to perfection and select a likely looking spot only to find the hatch has occurred elsewhere and once again you've backed the wrong horse. But if you wish to taste the cream of stillwater fly fishing then you must be prepared to take a risk, to gamble a few precious hours of your time. The rewards can be great

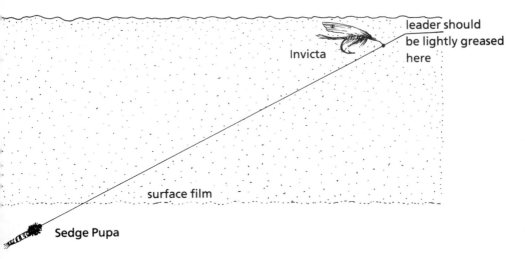

The perfect pair – the leader above the dropper should be lightly greased to keep the Invicta up near the surface while the Pupa is swimming a foot or two further down.

for the lucky angler who finds himself sharing a soft, summer evening with the pale, flickering forms of the sedge flies.

Lure Fishing

July is usually a marvellous month for lure fishing. Rainbows that have been waxing fat on the abundance of natural food since May are now at peak fitness and a fit rainbow is an aggressive fish.

No matter how committed an angler might be to nymphs and natural imitations he must accept that there are many occasions when a well fished lure will provide him with double the number of fish. I find this particularly true on those breezy, cloudy days that are so common in July, days when the sun is never behind a cloud long enough to encourage a proper hatch of flies and yet is never out long enough to drive the fish down into deep water. During the odd brief shady spell a few insects usually appear, keeping the fish active and in the mood to feed without ever preoccupying them. It is under these conditions that the lure can do great things for the skilled angler.

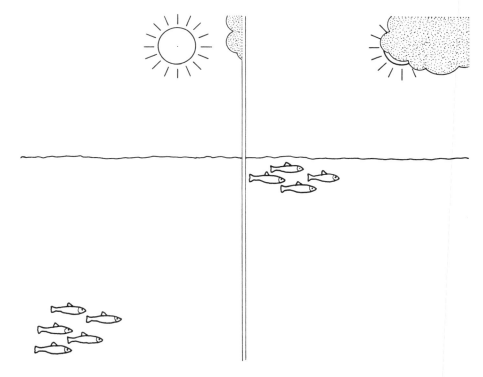

Bear in mind: the brighter the conditions, the deeper the fish are likely to be.

As always the angler's first problem is to find the fish and, as always, this will require some leg work. The shoals of rainbows will be smaller at this time of year and be wider spread which should give everyone a chance. Simply read the signs as we discussed earlier and sooner or later you'll find a few fish. By the way, if all else fails try to be around when your fishery staff top up with fresh stockies. This tends to liven up the resident fish who begin to move and betray their position.

Once the fish have been found then the real work can begin. Remember, you'll need to alter the depth at which you are fishing by a few feet every time the sun comes out from behind a cloud. Just keep it in mind that the brighter the conditions, the deeper the fish are likely to be.

As regards the fly itself, to a large degree I'll leave that choice to you. We all have our favourites. On the whole I prefer to stick with marabou lures and always carry a few black, white, orange and yellow patterns. Marabou is a beautiful material with an incredibly lifelike action when fished slowly. The problem is that very few anglers seem able to fish lures in any other way than at high speed. And yet there is no point in using marabou unless you're going to give the feather a chance to work. So why not try a gentle, irregular retrieve? Make the fly pulse and twitch through the water – and don't wait to feel the offers. Watch the line, and if it moves unnaturally, tighten up!

TWO FLIES FOR JULY

Sedge Flies

Trying to predict with any accuracy when one particular family of insects will begin hatching is virtually impossible. But it is reasonable to say that across most of the country sedge flies are unlikely to be seen in any quantity much before the middle of June. In my part of the world, the Midlands, it's more likely to be the beginning of July. It depends very much upon the weather for sedges are essentially creatures of high summer.

My two flies for this month are both sedge patterns and, in my opinion, are the perfect pair. I can never think of one without the other springing to mind. They go together like peaches and cream, or rhubarb and custard. I'm referring to the Sedge Pupa and that inspired creation of James Ogden, the Invicta. Now here are two flies that really are a bit 'special'. They're ideal for fishing as a pair and absolutely deadly when it comes to catching trout on soft, warm summer evenings when the sedges are on the wing.

How to Fish Them

See the main section on 'Tactics' in the general advice given for July (pages 52–4).

The Sedge Pupa

HOOK: Partridge Emerger Nymph GRS12ST, size 12.
THREAD: Brown.
BODY: A mix of yellow and orange seal's fur or substitute.
THORAX: Mid brown seal's fur or substitute.
RIB: Copper wire (fine).
WING CASE: Pheasant tail.

There are any number of different tyings for this particular pattern. My own version, which you are about to get, is as easy as any of them to put together. Simply wind on a layer of silk along the shank of the hook from eye to bend and back, and tie in a little lead. Then take the thread back down to the bend, nipping in the copper wire as you go. Now begin dubbing on the seal's fur substitute (I prefer a mix of 75 per cent yellow to 25 per cent orange) and build up a rather plump body. Overwind this fairly tightly with the rib and tie in the slip of pheasant tail that will act as the wing case. All you do now is dub on the thorax, then lay the wing case in position before tying off. And there it is, a juicy Sedge Pupa.

The Invicta

HOOK: Partridge Captain Hamilton LA2, size 10/12/14.
THREAD: Light brown.
TAIL: Golden pheasant crest feather.
RIB: Oval gold.
BODY: Yellow seal's fur or substitute.
BODY HACKLE: Red game cock.
WINGS: Hen pheasant tail.
THROAT-HACKLE: Fibres from the wing of a blue jay.

Lay down the usual base of tying thread from eye to bend, catching in the rib as you go. Next tie in a few tail fibres. Then dub on the body material and build up a nice slim profile, working back towards the eye. Remember not to go too far – you must leave sufficient room for winging. Time now to tie in the body hackle. Fix it firmly in position before winding it back down the body of the fly to the tail. The feather can be held in place by suspending a pair of hackle pliers from its tip while the rib is wound on in the opposite direction. This has the effect of trapping the hackle feather against the body of the fly and protecting it against the ravages of the trout's teeth. When the ribbing has been finished tie off. Winging the fly comes next and is probably the most difficult part of the whole operation. Slips cut from the centre tail feather of a hen bird was Ogden's original recommendation and who am I to argue? I would simply add that the younger the bird the better. Feather fibres from an ageing pheasant have an infuriating habit of splitting and separating, making a proper job almost impossible. Once the winging is complete add a sparse beard of blue jay, making sure the fibres are spread evenly and not tied in a clump. Finish by trimming off the waste ends and whipping a nice neat head.

THINGS TO REMEMBER
෴ JULY ෴

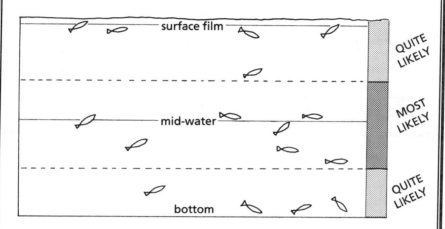

Fish Depth Guide – July

Water temperature   Very warm.

Fly hatches   Hatches of buzzers will be noticeably reduced this month and although the upwinged flies will still be in evidence they too will probably be on the decrease. Fortunately sedge flies are now beginning to appear in numbers, offering anglers the possibility of exciting fishing after the sun has gone down.

Fish behaviour   During the early part of the month there is still likely to be plenty of fish activity on or near the surface on cloudy, dull days. This need not be directly linked to feeding. Rainbows in particular are prone to bouts of 'sporting' during these warmer months, often hurling themselves clear of the water. Serious feeding, however, tends to be confined to dawn and dusk.

Fly selection   Although the Damsel Nymph will continue to reap rich rewards this month, it is the appearance of the sedge flies that is of most significance to the angler. A Sedge

Pupa (size 12) fished as a point fly, with an Invicta (sizes 14 to 10) on the dropper, make a perfect pair for dealing with an evening hatch of sedges.

Retrieve Unlike most natural imitations the Sedge Pupa and Invicta are best fished fairly briskly. I find steady pulls of twelve inches to be best for this purpose.

Conditions on the day If you intend to fish a full day during July then you'd best pray for a dull one. Overcast conditions offer the angler a chance of good sport – overcast windy conditions are even better. But if the weather turns out to be bright and calm you'd do better to focus your efforts on the periods of dawn and dusk.

❧ AUGUST ❧

GENERAL ADVICE

The Dog-Days

Ever since my first pathetic attempts to cast a fly all those years ago I have been listening to warnings about the awful month of August. Other more experienced anglers warned me, the angling papers warned me, every fishing book I read (and I read a great many in those days) repeated the warning. And yet, if I remember correctly, the dog-days arrived early and unannounced that first season, thanks to a blazingly hot July, and I found that in my ignorance I'd fished through them without knowing. August turned out to be a dull, wet month that left me feeling rather let down.

Perhaps, before we go any further, I ought to define that old angling term 'dog-days' for the benefit of anyone who hasn't yet come across it. A dog-day refers to the worst possible set of conditions that we anglers can face – blazing sunshine, clear blue skies and not a breath of wind to relieve the monotony. In other words, perfect sunbathing weather.

I can't remember learning very much that first season but, if nothing else, it taught me that it is naive to expect these conditions only to occur in August. They can happen at any time between June and September. So why is it August has such a bad name? Probably because in an average year (if there is such a thing) the rapidly rising air temperatures of early summer often lead to a wet and stormy July which, most people feel, should be followed by a hot and sunny August. The problem of course with these sorts of predictions is that very often a wet and windy July is followed by a wet and windy August, which is followed by a wet and windy September, etc.

And so my advice is to take August as it comes, without prejudice. Sure, there are bound to be a few dog-days, but there will also be overcast days that offer fishing as good as almost any other month. You'll notice I qualified that statement by using the word 'almost'. You see there *is* something a little odd about August, something not quite right, something that sets it apart from the other summer months. Yet try as I might I've never really been able to put my finger on it. Most of the usual flies will hatch, though not as prolifically as earlier in the year, and the fish will also feed, though not quite as vigorously as one might expect. It's as if nature has stopped briefly to rest after her exertions climbing the hill of spring and summer, using August as a plateau on which to pause and draw breath before plunging headlong downwards into September and October. I can't put it any more precisely than that I'm afraid.

Alright then, let's begin bravely by looking at the worst conditions we will face and what effect they will have on our fishing. It is a fact that bright hot weather makes fly fishing difficult for everyone. But it is the bank angler who suffers most. Weed will have been growing at a tremendous rate over the past few weeks making many shallow areas of water virtually unfishable, while at the same time the trout are being driven into the cooler, deeper reaches that are often out of casting range from the bank. High temperatures suck oxygen from the water leaving it flat and warm, like stale beer, and a lack of wind makes the already reluctant fish even less likely to come to a fly that, no matter how carefully cast, seems to fall like a depth charge into the glassy surface of the pool, setting up ripples that reach the far shore.

The only sensible thing to do under these circumstances is to restrict your activity to early mornings and late evenings when the trout are likely to be in a rather more cooperative mood. However, if you're feeling particularly masochistic and decide to take on August at its worst, I can do no better than suggest you turn back a few pages to June's chapter and follow the instructions on fishing the Booby Nymph to the letter. But be under no illusion – any fish taken under these conditions will have been hard earned.

Blessing or Curse?

If conditions are as we like them, with some cloud and a forgiving breeze, those rafts of weed that have grown to become such a nuisance over the past few weeks can now prove more of a blessing than a curse to the bank angler. Not only do they offer precious cover to the trout, they also contain a considerable amount of insect life. In fact they're a veritable treasure chest of food. Even the shoals of coarse fry that are so abundant at this time of year will be found taking refuge in and around this watery undergrowth. It's hardly surprising therefore that the trout will spend much of their time foraging amongst these weed banks. Even if the weather has been extremely hot and bright, it is to the weedy margins that they will return as darkness approaches. For the angler it's simply a case of being patient.

Food Sources

We can still expect to see enough insects hatching on most days to keep the fish active, even though this activity may only be spasmodic. For the early part of the month we'll be relying quite heavily on buzzers and damsel nymphs during the daytime, and hoping that the sedges will put in an appearance at dusk. The other important food source in August is the one referred to earlier, the coarse fry. Although September is recognized as *the* month for capturing the 'fry feeders', it is, in fact, usually August when the trout seem to become suddenly aware of this handy source of protein. It is more than likely that this cannibalistic behaviour is encouraged by the steady decline in insect life at this time of year and that the fish are simply supplementing one food source for another. (For fry feeding see September, page 71.)

Spotting the Fish

Spotting the fish in heavily weeded areas is not as difficult as one might think, provided we understand how they are feeding and what we should be looking for. It's easy enough to spot a fish that rises and takes a fly from the surface but these 'weed feeders' spend most of their time cruising along the outer edges of the underwater vegetation in search of fly larvae, nymphs, *Corixa* and such like. This kind of feeding is a leisurely business compared to a proper rise when the trout are competing for food on or near the surface. But if the fish makes a sudden

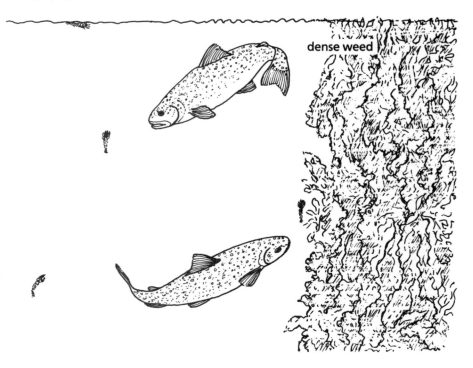

If a fish makes a sudden turn or rises quickly from near the bottom, the water displacement will cause tiny ripples to appear alongside the weed.

turn, or rises quickly from near the bottom, the water displacement will cause tiny ripples to appear alongside the weed, making it rock gently, even though the fish may not have broken surface. Don't expect this water disturbance to be at all violent – it won't be, so you'll need to be observant and to have your wits about you.

Tactics

You should start your search for the fish on those banks that are fringed by a ribbon of weed no more than seven or eight feet wide. One of the controlling factors of weed growth is water depth and you'll usually find that on the far side of the weed bank the lake bed falls away quite steeply. Once your target area has been selected don't pull on your waders and go plunging in thoughtlessly, frightening every fish inside a half mile radius. Instead spend five minutes sitting quietly, watching for any of the signs we discussed earlier. And don't be too downhearted if there are no immediate indications that there are fish nearby. An absence of signs doesn't always equate to an absence of trout!

While sitting and watching why not have a think about what fly you intend to use? My preference would be for one of my own nymph patterns on one rod and an Appetizer on the other. Fortunately for the

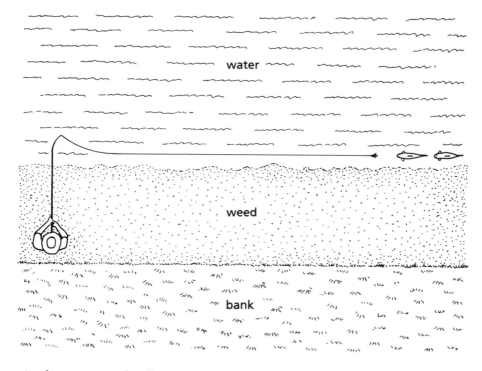

Angler retrieving his fly alongside a weed bed.

angler these 'weed feeders' develop fairly catholic tastes and are as likely to take one well fished fly as another. Floating lines are a must for this kind of fishing and I'd advise you to stick to only one fly on the cast. It's difficult enough dragging a hooked fish through heavy weed without having droppers snagging in the process. It would also be foolhardy to use a point of less than 5 lb breaking strain, for when you hook the fish there will be no time for fancy tactics and looking good. It will be a case of hit him and hold hard!

I would suggest you begin fishing with fairly short casts (playing a fish on a long line near weed beds is asking for trouble) made parallel with the bank. Aim to drop your fly a yard out into clear water. Then, with your rod tip protruding out past the overgrown area, begin your retrieve. The object of the exercise is to search the edge of the weed bank with your fly swimming a couple of feet down. It has been my experience that any deep-lying fish are usually prepared to rise up to intercept the fly as it passes overhead. If an offer is received and the fish is hooked it really is a case of giving as little line as possible unless he decides to fight it out in open water. This happens surprisingly often and I'll never understand why, with the refuge of a weed bed only feet away, the trout

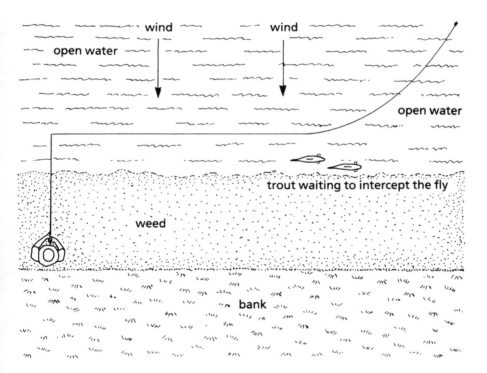

When the wind is blowing directly into the bank, try casting further out into the lake and allowing a bow to develop in the line.

should elect to carry the battle into open water. It makes me think that if they were only half as cunning as chub we'd never get them out.

As always the retrieve is critical and if the fish won't come to a steady figure of eight then try a slow sink and draw. One method to be avoided is that where the angler tucks the rod under one arm and retrieves hand over hand. This may work for you in open water but under these conditions that momentary loss of control as you transfer the rod back to hand could be disastrous.

When the wind is blowing directly into the bank, a tactic I've found useful, particularly with lures, is to cast the fly a little further out into the lake and allow a bow to develop in the line. When the line at the centre of the bow is about to touch the weed I begin a slow retrieve. Then, as the fly swings in towards the weed, I accelerate the retrieve progressively, causing it to come swooping in at a sharp angle to the bank. The take, which is usually very positive, is likely to come as the fly picks up speed.

This kind of 'close quarter' angling is more akin to hunting than fishing and therein lies the charm of it. We're not fishing the water in the true sense, we're actually searching for the fish. Over the years many good trout have fallen to my rod using these tactics and yet each time my fly is taken, whether it is signalled by the line being drawn gently down into the water or suddenly snapping taut as a fish takes at speed, my heart still jumps in my chest. The surprise and delight of it all is something I've never quite grown used to.

An Alternative for August

Some years ago, on a lovely warm late summer afternoon, I paid a visit to a small day-ticket water not far from my home. Although the day was fairly bright there was still enough of a breeze to corrugate the surface of the water with a steady ripple and on arrival I fully expected to see some action. However, after circling the pool looking in vain for signs of fish or fly, I began to fear the worst. The water appeared lifeless. Then, for no obvious reason, the odd fish began topping in an area where a high sandy bank kept the wind from the surface of the water, creating a band of calm some twenty yards wide. The trout were feeding splashily right on the edge of this, just where the calm water met the ripple. I scuttled back along the bank, hoping that the action would not be short lived and that I'd at least have the chance of a cast or two.

In fact I needn't have hurried for the rise took on a steady pattern with fish showing regularly, though I couldn't for the life of me see what they were feeding on. I dropped a Damsel Nymph in amongst them several times, never once receiving an offer. Then for a few moments the wind eased and the insects that were being blown off the high bank behind me began to fall much closer in. They were ants, flying ants, and it didn't take me long to discover their source. The ground was riddled with ants' nests and the surrounding area alive with the winged insects. As I watched several of them took to the air and were instantly caught by the breeze that had sprung up again and whisked out over the water to where the trout were once more having a beanfeast.

I moved back down to the water's edge, debating what fly to fish (for in those days I didn't carry an ant imitation), eventually settling for a little Black and Peacock Spider. This did not bring immediate success and it was only after a little surgery had been performed on the hackle with a pair of scissors that the first offer came, a thump that I felt down in my boots. The fish ran long and hard, though not very fast, and took a full fly line before the side strain I was applying finally turned him. He came kiting around in a huge half circle, only to set off in the opposite direction, the line whistling like a bosun.

The battle, which lasted several minutes, was stately rather than exciting, with the fish developing plenty of torque but at fairly low revs, and it was only necessary for me to be patient to be assured of success. After what seemed an eternity I slipped the net under a beautifully proportioned fish in excess of five pounds. Now I know that this is not particularly remarkable but when I tell you that, on the very next cast, I hooked and landed a twin to that first fish, you can see why I have such a soft spot for the humble Ant. Two five pounders in consecutive casts is a feat I've never repeated. Since that day I make sure that when August arrives, no matter where I'm fishing, my fly box contains a number of proper Ant patterns. Like the crane flies, it is a terrestrial insect we can rely upon to put in an appearance over the next few weeks.

TWO FLIES FOR AUGUST

The Appetizer

This excellent lure was first tied by Bob Church way back in 1973 and has since established itself as a favourite among stillwater trout anglers. It is one of those patterns, like the Marabou Viva, that you can depend upon regardless of where you might be fishing.

Although I suspect that Bob tied the Appetizer originally as a fry pattern (the white marabou wing overlaid by squirrel tail fibres points to that), it didn't take anglers long to recognize its value as an 'all-rounder'. Indeed at this time of the year, when those microscopic crustaceans we know as *Daphnia* are hatching in their millions, I have found this fly to be an absolute killer.

How to Fish It

Like all light coloured flies I prefer to fish the Appetizer high in the water on floating or intermediate lines. The leader can be a fairly simple affair – a seven foot butt section of 10 lb breaking strain nylon onto which is tied a further eight foot length of 5 lb breaking strain. This is the business end. Whatever you do don't be tempted to go below a point of 5 lb breaking strain. This lure should be fished quite briskly and 'crash takes' are not exactly uncommon. It's not the loss of the fish that concerns me so much as the thought of the poor creature trailing several yards of nylon line behind it.

Precision casting, nice though it is, isn't really necessary when we are searching the water rather than casting to individual fish. By all means select a target, a particular spot on the surface, and do your best to put your fly within a foot or two of it. But don't worry too much if you miss the bull's-eye and only score an inner. Take comfort from the knowledge that this target practice will be improving your accuracy for the future.

Tying Instructions

HOOK: Partridge Bucktail Streamer D4A, size 8/10.
THREAD: White.
TAIL AND THROAT: Mixed orange and green hackle fibres.
BODY: White chenille.
RIB: Silver tinsel.
WING: White marabou overlaid by natural grey squirrel tail.

Put down a nice even base of tying silk along the hook shank in the usual manner and tie in a little lead for ballast as you go. When you've done that take the thread back towards the bend and catch in the rib. Now fix the tail fibres and, at the same time, tie in securely one end of your chenille wool. OK so far? Good. You can now take the tying silk back up to the eye of the hook and follow it with the chenille in neat, touching turns. The body profile should be slim and streamlined. Next wind on the rib in easy open turns and tie off. To fix the throat hackle turn the fly over in the vice and attach a few wisps of the tail material. You won't need much. Just sufficient to give a tinge of colour. Then, with the fly once more in the upright position, tie in the wing, overlaying it with a few squirrel tail fibres. Once again these should be kept to a minimum or they will inhibit the action of the marabou when the fly is being fished. Finish off with a nicely proportioned head and a dab of varnish.

The Flying Ant

Patterns tied to represent this particular insect are many and varied. Unfortunately very few of them can be fished up in the surface film for any period of time without the use of artificial floatant, something I detest. As a consequence I set about designing my own winged ant. It took a little thought and there were quite a few failures but the end result was a fly that did everything I asked of it.

How to Fish It

Fishing a winged ant is similar in many ways to fishing a dry fly, the essential difference being that the ant should hang suspended in the surface film rather than sitting high and dry on top of it. As always presentation is the key to success. On land the ant is a tremendously robust creature, strong and resourceful, but as an aviator it is strictly second class and very much at the mercy of the wind when airborne. As a swimmer too it would win no prizes, especially when weighed down by wings that appear to have been made for an insect at least twice its size. It was this thought that gave me a useful pointer when creating my 'new' fly. The movements of the ant when caught up in the surface film are so feeble that they can't be imitated accurately by any of the normal retrieve styles. Consequently it is better not to retrieve the fly at all but to rely on wind and wave power to give the fly life and movement. Fortunately wind and the arrival of terrestrials on the water usually coincide. To overcome the problem of suspending the artificial for long periods in the surface film I began using a buoyant polyfoam wing. This is the flat foam material used as protective packing for delicate goods. Not only is it pleasant to work with, it will also float all day without ever becoming waterlogged.

Fishing this pattern couldn't be easier. Once the fish have shown themselves, and you have established that they are feeding on ants, just cast your artificial as near as possible to the centre of activity and wait for a response. The fly, suspended only by the polyfoam wing, will be extremely difficult to pick out at distance, especially if the water is choppy. It's necessary therefore to concentrate on movement of the fly line to signal when a fish has taken it. That twelve inches between the rod tip and the water is the best bite indicator under these circumstances. You should respond to any movement of this short section, no matter how slight, by tightening up. By the way, the line won't always pull away from you. A sudden slackening of pressure is just as likely to indicate a fish taking hold.

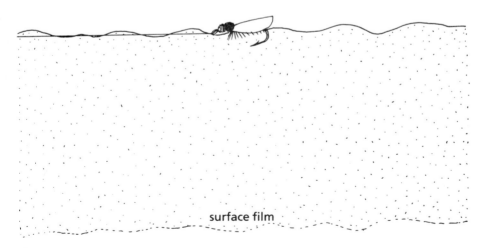

surface film

The Flying Ant pattern should hang suspended in the surface film rather than sit high and dry on top of it.

Tying Instructions

HOOK: Partridge Down Eye Dry Fly E6A, size 12/14.
THREAD: Black.
BODY: Black seal's fur substitute.
HACKLE: Black cock.
WING: Flat polyfoam.

Begin by taking the tying thread neatly from the eye of the hook down to the bend. Then, with the last couple of turns, tie in by its tip a small black hackle feather. Now dub on the seal's fur substitute and build up a gently swelling body that should occupy approximately two-thirds of the hook shank, working back towards the eye. Don't bother to tie off yet. Just leave the thread dangling on the bobbin. Now take the hackle feather and wind it two or three times around the body, no more than that. It's very easy to spoil this pattern by over-dressing. At this point you can tie off the hackle and cut away the excess feather.

The time has now come to fashion the wing. Nothing could be simpler, believe me. Just cut out a largish diamond shape of polyfoam and tie it in by one corner so that the remainder slopes back over the body of the fly. Finish off with a large, nicely formed head and the usual dab of varnish, then trim the wing to its final shape when this is dry.

THINGS TO REMEMBER
✑ AUGUST ✑

Water temperature   At its highest for the year.

Fly hatches   Hatches of aquatic insects are now in steady decline. Sedges will continue to put in an appearance as darkness approaches but the buzzers and upwinged flies are unlikely to be seen in quantity this month. There will, however, be a number of terrestrial insects around, two of which are of interest to the angler. These are the flying ant and the crane fly.

Fish behaviour   Trout can be perverse creatures during high summer, hiding away for much of the time in deep water and only rising to feed with the approach of darkness. But don't despair altogether. Any odd period of wet and windy weather is likely to stimulate them into feeding and could make daytime angling a worthwhile bet.

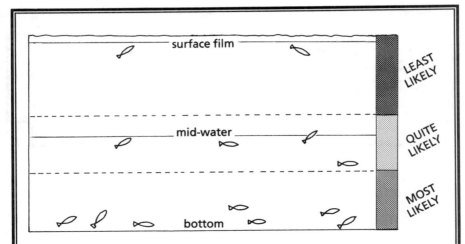

Fish Depth Guide – August

Fly selection   An excellent all-round lure pattern is the Appetizer (sizes 8/10). I find it especially effective during the warmer months of the year when water temperatures are relatively high. My Flying Ant imitation (size 12/14) is a good copy of one of the major terrestrial insects that is likely to influence the behaviour of the trout this month.

Retrieve   Let's deal with the ant pattern first. This fly doesn't require retrieving. Just make the cast and leave the wind and the waves to impart life. If you can't see the fly then watch the line closely for unusual movement that might signify a trout taking hold. The Appetizer requires a quite different approach. It is best fished high in the water with a brisk figure of eight or a snappy pull and pause retrieve.

Conditions on the day   A simple message for August: avoid the 'dog-days' if at all possible. There is little to be gained by fishing in heat-wave conditions. But be ready to make the most of any periods of rough or squally weather. Other than that it's still early mornings and late evenings, I'm afraid!

SEPTEMBER

GENERAL ADVICE

During the spring green years of my childhood each day seemed to last a week and a year was a lifetime in which babies were born, old people died, wars were won and monarchs crowned. Later, when I reached the plateau of early manhood, I was so convinced of my own immortality that I gave the passage of time no thought at all. There was just too much to do. A pretty girl to marry, a career to forge and children to raise. It is only recently, with the arrival of middle age and my family grown up, that time has begun to accelerate. Weeks merge one into the other and the months are flying past. It seems only yesterday that I was fishing through the cold, blustery days of early spring with numbed fingers and streaming eyes, pining for the warmth and activity of May and June, and yet, as I sit here at my desk, the calendar on the wall tells me that summer is already a thing of the past. My only consolation is that September is here and with it the loveliest season of all, autumn.

If I were to carry out a poll amongst anglers as to which was their favourite month of the year, September would win hands down, of that I have no doubt. Indeed it would probably be my own were it not for the thought of the season's end hovering like a spectre on the horizon. But what is it about this time of the year that makes it so startlingly different to any other? There is no single, simple answer to that question. To understand why most experienced anglers regard September so highly we must look at various factors that coincide quite naturally to provide what is potentially the most productive period of all for the fly fisher.

First, with high summer now behind us, water temperatures will be dropping quite quickly. The rain that so often greets this particular month simply accelerates the cooling process and with this drop in temperature will come an increase in fish activity. In case you weren't aware of it already, the trout, especially rainbows, are always fitter, happier and more active in cool water.

Secondly, although the usual aquatic flies will continue to hatch, their numbers will be declining. This is not quite the bad news that it might first appear, for fish that have been extremely selective in their feeding habits over the past two months should now come to our flies much more readily.

Thirdly, fish that have waxed fat on an abundance of insects during the summer will now have to work harder and seek alternative sources of food if they are to maintain their condition. These alternatives will include coarse fry and an increasing number of terrestrial insects.

And finally, I'm pretty sure that trout, like all other wild creatures, sense the passing of summer and the onset of winter. Their appetites will be sharp as they seek to take on as much energy as possible during September's shortening days, before the frosts of October arrive and nature begins to doze in the first stages of hibernation.

Fly Hatches (The Big Three)

Although the ubiquitous buzzer will still be in evidence on waters around the country, I would advise you to make the most of any hatches you come across, for September is likely to be the last month that buzzer patterns will do much damage to the trout stocks of our fisheries.

Sedges too will continue to emerge most evenings, unless of course temperatures begin to fall dramatically as does sometimes happen.

As for the olives, you may have noticed that they have been conspicuous by their absence during August. We can, however, expect them to reappear for one final fling in September and this is sure to be greeted enthusiastically by the trout, so don't be caught out. Make sure you have sufficient patterns in your fly box to deal with such an occasion.

Alternatives

As mentioned earlier, the general decline in fly hatches will, by now, have encouraged the trout to begin searching for other kinds of food. I'd like to spend the next few pages discussing two of these alternatives and their value to the bank angler.

Fish Fry

Probably the most significant change in the feeding habits of the trout occurs when they recognize the value of coarse fry as a source of protein. This cannibalistic behaviour will have begun last month but by September tiny fish will make up a large part of the trout's diet. Now this may be bad news for the fry (their existence will be a precarious one to say the least between now and next spring) but it's good news for the bank angler. Not only are fry feeding fish reasonably easy to tempt, they're also almost always within easy casting range as they forage around the margins in search of their prey. In fact it has been my experience that there are more fish close in to the bank in September

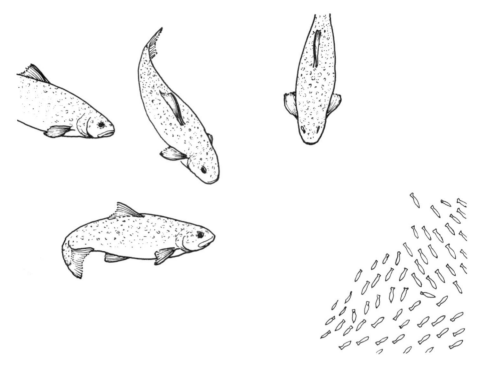

Rainbow trout work in packs like wolves, herding fry into shallow water until they are packed in tight against the bank.

than at any other time of the year, with the exception of early season when the initial heavy stocking takes place.

Before we go on to discuss flies and tactics for this kind of fishing we would do well to understand exactly what happens beneath the surface when the trout take it into their heads to savage the shoals of small perch, roach, rudd and bream that abound in most still waters.

Rainbow trout work in packs, like wolves, herding the fry into shallow water until they're packed tight against the bank. Then, at top speed, they come hurtling in, hurling themselves at the shoal, devouring some fish as they go and, at the same time, bruising and damaging many more. After the initial attack the area will be littered with tiny bodies suspended in mid water, some moving feebly, others still, all at the mercy of their assassins who come sliding quietly back in to finish the job, picking off the casualties at their leisure. For me this scene, more than any other, is a microcosm of nature's cruelty. And it's not only the rainbows who carry out this savagery. Big brownies that for most of the season have been virtually uncatchable will also be overcome in this fry feeding frenzy, and I regard September as possibly the best month of all for taking quality brown trout.

Artificials

There are almost as many fry patterns for the angler to choose from as there are weeks in the year and most of them will catch fish. Many people swear by a traditional pattern like a Missionary, others prefer something simple like one of the Baby Doll variation. 'And what about a Mylar Minnow?' I can hear someone at the back shouting. The only advice I can offer is that you should fish the fly in which you have most confidence. For those of you who can't make up their minds let me offer my own pattern with the hand on heart assurance that it also catches fish. I introduced it to the general public some years ago through one of the national angling magazines. My only mistake at the time was in not christening it. As a consequence it became known as the 'No Name' lure! (Tying instructions follow later.)

Tactics

Fry feeding is a pretty extravagant business and should not be too difficult for the observant angler to spot. We should be looking for any sudden or vigorous movement near the margins that is often preceded by dozens of tiny fish splintering the surface as they leap for their lives. Should you be lucky enough to spot this kind of activity please don't go rushing along the bank until you're standing over that very spot. Approach stealthily, keeping low, and at all costs avoid being silhouetted against the skyline. Although the trout may appear to be in a feeding frenzy a large dark shape lurching into view will soon put

Tiny fish splinter the surface as they leap for their lives!

them down. On the other hand they don't seem adversely affected by the thrashing of a hooked fish, possibly because of the violent movement already taking place amongst the others.

A floating line is essential when fishing this close to the bank. Remember to wet the fly thoroughly before you begin and keep false casting to a minimum. If you're using my pattern give it two or three seconds after the cast has been made before you begin your retrieve, keeping a sharp eye open for offers that might come 'on the drop'. The 'No Name' is taken in this fashion quite regularly. Obviously the trout take it for a damaged fish when they see it sinking slowly through the water, that marabou wing fluttering temptingly.

The retrieve should be started with the rod tip held a couple of feet above the water and with the rod itself at ninety degrees to the line. These precautions are simply to avoid the fly being cracked off by a fish taking at speed, a common enough occurrence with fry feeding trout. I know that there are various 'stretchy' materials on the market nowadays but after suffering problems setting the hook I am reluctant to recommend them. I find that extra foot of loose line and the natural spring of the rod tip does the job just as well.

The real fascination in this type of fishing comes with trying to imitate the struggles of the injured fish. I find that five or six short pulls that cause the fly to rise jerkily to the surface, followed by a good long pause that allows the fly to sink again, can be deadly. A normal fast retrieve will also be effective but it has its drawbacks, the obvious one being that the fly is not in the killing area for very long. But whatever style you employ you'll need to work fast for fry feeding trout don't stay in exactly the same place for too long. After a couple of attacks the fry will have scattered, taking the trout with them, so it's important to take full advantage of any action you may find. Then it's a case of beginning the search all over again.

Fishing a fry pattern should not be written off as merely 'lure bashing'. If carried out properly it is as much a genuinely imitative form of fishing as using a nymph or dry fly. However, if you're happier sticking with nymphs and happen one day to come across a shoal of fry feeding trout, don't hesitate. Mount the largest pattern you have in your box on a point of at least 5 lb breaking strain and fish it with an irregular figure of eight retrieve. You could be surprised by the results.

The Crane Fly

My second alternative for September is another terrestrial insect. If God created a clumsier, more ungainly insect than the crane fly I haven't come across it yet. Known universally as the daddy longlegs, there are over three hundred species in Britain alone, the largest of which grows to a length exceeding one inch. It is a creature that raises terror in the breast of most ladies (the mere sight of one indoors is enough to have my wife packing her bags) but is regarded as manna from heaven by fly fishers everywhere. Although some species put in an appearance as early as May the majority of adult flies won't be with us until August or September. At times the sheer volume of them can be staggering. I have walked across fields so blackened with their bodies that the grass appeared scorched and each footfall raised dense clouds of them.

The crane fly is one of the very few terrestrial insects to generate a proper rise from the trout. Certainly any insect is likely to be eaten if it falls onto the surface of the water but, by and large, these are individual incidents when patrolling fish come across the creature struggling to free itself and snap it up. Crane flies, on the other hand, can provide a rather more dramatic response. Their numbers are such that if only five per cent of their total is carried by the wind from the surrounding countryside onto the water it is enough to have every trout in the vicinity up on the surface within minutes, mouths open, lolloping about like schoolboys in a tuck shop. This is understandable, of course. The daddy is a big insect, a real mouthful for the fish who, like most of God's creatures, prefers to take in as much as possible in one bite.

Tactics

The tactics I employ when fishing a crane fly pattern are fairly straightforward. Although accuracy and speed of casting are not things I have demanded from you up to this point, they are just what are required now. This need for precision will soon become clear. The trout are liable to be travelling fast when they begin to reap this unexpected harvest from the surface. If we can judge the direction of their route we can put the artificial in the right place at the right time. Care should be taken, however, not to over-cast. It's better that the fly should fall short than you disturb the fish by dropping yards of heavy fly line on its head.

Once the fly is out there you can expect an offer at any time. You could be lucky and see it disappear immediately in the heavy swirl caused by a trout sucking it down, but if it's not taken in the first ten seconds then you're better off moving it. Use short, smooth pulls to drag it down just below the surface and continue twitching it back through the water. Now I know that crane flies don't behave in that fashion, and of course trout should not pursue them and grab hold, but they do! Ask anyone who fishes this pattern regularly and they'll confirm it. Takes are usually quite bold – a boil followed by a sharp snatch is what mostly happens, so try not to strike too firmly. Just lift the rod and let the fish do the rest.

A UNIVERSAL PROBLEM

All anglers lose fish. That is a fact of fishing and always will be. There are things, however, that we can do to shorten the odds in our favour. But first we need to understand *why* the problem occurs, and, in almost every case, the answer is the same. The fish is lost because the hook fails to gain proper purchase in the fish's mouth. Obvious? Yes of course, but what is not quite so clear is why.

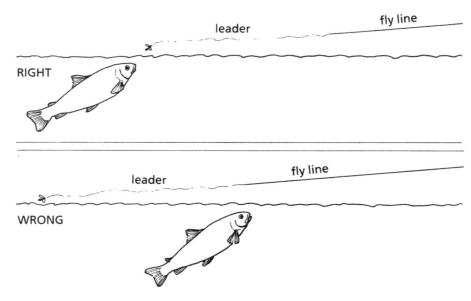

Care should be taken not to over-cast. It's better the fly should fall short than the fish be disturbed by dropping yards of heavy fly line on its head!

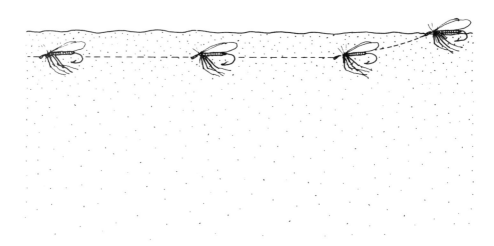

If the Crane Fly is not taken in the first ten seconds then you're better off moving it. Use short, smooth pulls to drag it beneath the surface.

The most common cause of lack of hook penetration is simply that the hook is not sharp. It may have been when you started your day's fishing but a fly takes a hell of a bashing in just an hour and it's the easiest thing in the world to roll over that needle point on a stone in shallow water, or even on a fish's jaw.

I never cease to be amazed at the number of anglers who hook and lose a fish then continue fishing without ever checking their hook. Every time – and I mean *every* time – you hook and lose a fish you should check the condition of your hook before re-casting. Not just a quick glance but a real inspection. And yet it happens again and again. In the heat of battle even experienced anglers have been known to forget this basic discipline and I have watched friends of mine lose anything up to three fish before discovering that the hook had broken on the bend.

Playing a fish too hard is also a recipe for disaster. It's not that the line will break but more likely that the hook will pull through that bit of skin that is so often all that connects you to the fish.

There are also the times when the fish feed only tentatively, nipping at the tail of the fly rather than taking it fully into their mouths – 'coming short' is the old expression. Flies with long marabou tails are very prone to this sort of fast, pecking offer. And if you attempt to improve your chances by shortening the tail the bites cease altogether. One way around this problem is to switch to a pattern with a marabou wing. The feather is then long enough to remain attractive to the fish but the hook point is nearer the back end of the fly which should result in a higher percentage of solid takes.

Unfortunately there are also times when, no matter how much care we take, or how sharp our hooks are, the fish still escape with dreadful regularity. And so, for occasions like this, here's a tip I was given many

UPRIGHT

HORIZONTAL

Look closely at your fly in the water and make sure it is swimming in the upright position.

years ago by an elderly gentleman who taught me a great deal in a very short space of time. Look closely at your fly in the water and make sure it is swimming in the upright position. In other words, that it is in the vertical plane. If the fly is swimming on its side when the fish takes it into its mouth there is a very good chance you'll pull it straight out again on the strike. At best you're only likely to gain the minimum hook hold which will almost certainly give under pressure.

What causes the fly to swim in the horizontal plane rather than the vertical? It's usually a case of bad dressing, bushier on one side than the other. This can be overcome to some degree by adjusting the hackle or plucking out a few body fibres to counteract that bushy effect. What cannot be rectified, however, is a fly that has been weighted unevenly. No amount of dress adjustment will overcome the built in bias. You'd be better off throwing it into the bin or, if you tie your own flies, stripping it down and saving the hook for future use.

TWO FLIES FOR SEPTEMBER

The 'No Name' Lure

I designed this pattern originally for one of my local waters, a place that had more than its fair share of roach and rudd. This accounts for the three basic colours of cream, white and orange. Let me say right away that, as a fry pattern, it is very successful. But it was a close friend of mine, someone who fishes with me most weekends, who discovered that this fly had an additional 'special' quality.

We were out on a typically cold, early season day with nothing much happening, both of us fishing large leaded nymphs on slow sinking lines. With mechanical thoroughness we flogged our way along stretches of shoreline hoping some unseen stockie would cooperate and grab hold. It was no more scientific than that. By lunchtime I had persuaded two fish to come to the net but my friend had blanked. We then stopped for a bite to eat before splitting up, he going one way and I the other. We didn't see each other again until the end of the day. I was feeling particularly pleased with myself after winkling out another five smallish rainbows, but he soon wiped the smile from my face. He'd taken only five fish but all were in excess of two pounds with the biggest a couple of ounces over five! Not bad for an ordinary day-ticket water. All had come to the fly he calls 'the roach pattern'.

If this had been a one-off I'd not have bothered mentioning it but for the next six weeks he fished with virtually nothing else on his line and had some really splendid bags. He also had the impudence to repeat his performance with the five pounder – twice!

As far as we could tell none of the fish he caught were feeding on fry. At least there had been none of the usual crashing and splashing associated with trout beating up the fry and there were certainly no small fish inside them. Yet they had been persuaded to take this fly after refusing most others. That fascinated me. My friend, on the other hand, has a far more pragmatic approach to his fishing. As far as he was concerned the 'roach pattern' caught fish, big fish too, and that was all that mattered. Even so I still wasn't convinced and so we set about putting his beliefs to the test. We did this by first finding a few trout, then fished for them hard with flies we knew we could count on before switching to the No Name. The results, in almost every case, were the same. The bigger specimens came to the roach pattern. It really does seem to be a fly that has that extra bit of magic that tempts the heavyweights.

How to Fish It

Although this fly has proved itself capable of catching fish almost any time, I tend to use it more as a 'special', a tool for specific occasions. When the trout are feeding on fry is only one such occasion. There are others – for example, those days when the rainbow shoals become aggressively active, not feeding in the true sense but sporting themselves, rising suddenly from several feet down and either jumping or rolling noisily on the surface. Just thinking about it makes my pulse rate increase. Conditions like that will always have me reaching into my fly box for a No Name lure. This fly, fished on a floating or intermediate line and twitched through a few feet down, can produce the kind of thumping offers that have been known to snatch the line from unsuspecting fingers, so be on your guard. That reminds me, it is not advisable to use a point of less than 5 lb breaking strain when casting to 'sporting' fish. They do grab hold very aggressively.

Another time when I'm particularly happy to fish this pattern is when the weather is bright and sunny. I have invariably found a light coloured fly to be best in really bright conditions and the No Name has a bit of a twinkle that looks good under water.

And finally, with regard to this lure's ability to tempt the larger fish, if you're catching regularly from one spot using another fly, why not take a gamble and give this roach pattern twenty minutes of the session? It could well reward you with the biggest fish of the day.

There are many things in my life that, in retrospect, I regret. One of them is the fact that I did not give this fly a name. As a result of my laziness it is now stuck with the title 'No Name', such an ugly term for such a pretty fly.

Tying Instructions

HOOK: Partridge Grey Shadow GRS4A, size 8/10.
THREAD: White.
TAIL AND THROAT: Fire orange wool.
BODY: Cream seal's fur substitute.
RIB: Silver tinsel.
WING: White marabou.

Begin by putting down the usual neat bed of tying silk along the hook shank from eye to bend and back again. Then layer on your lead to suit and tie it in as you take the thread back down to the bend. Now tie in a stubby tail of the fire orange wool while, at the same time, nipping in your rib. The rest is fairly straightforward. Dub on the body material and build up a nice slim profile, working your way back towards the eye. Follow this with the ribbing and tie off. All that's left now is to fix the wing in position. By the way, try not to over-dress at this point. It's easily done using marabou. Just before finishing off the head of the fly catch in a few fibres of the orange wool at the throat, just enough to give a blush of colour. And there you have it. Another fly with no name!

The Crane Fly

There can be very few artificials more fun to fish than the crane fly. It is one of those patterns that can lie unused in a corner of your fly box for months on end, simply occupying space. But you can be certain that the first time you dare go fishing without a few 'daddies' will be the time you need them most. It's called 'Sod's Law'!

How to Fish It

Crane fly artificials should always be fished on a floating line. I like a leader of around fifteen feet graduated down to a point of 4 lb breaking strain. Before beginning to fish it is important that the last five or six feet of leader is thoroughly de-greased. The reason for this will become clear as we go along.

When trout begin rising to take aquatic flies from the surface it is often a gradual process. They will have followed the main body of insects as they rose from the lake bed, feeding on them as they struggle upwards. It is for that reason that visible activity in the beginning is slow, increasing only gradually as the bulk of the hatch nears the surface.

But when the trout start to feed on terrestrial insects this development stage of the rise doesn't take place. There is no underwater build-up. Subsequently the angler has little or no warning of what is about to happen. It is important therefore that we identify the cause of the rise as soon as possible for once the last fly is taken from the surface the trout will disappear just as quickly as they arrived.

Fortunately, daddy longlegs are easily spotted. It's then a case of putting up an artificial straightaway and doing your best to cast it into the path of a feeding fish. Predicting the route a trout is taking is really not that difficult provided you concentrate on one fish and watch carefully. However, if the fly isn't taken in the first few seconds (à la dry fly) then do as I suggested earlier and pull it back sub-surface. This is where those few feet of de-greased leader come into play.

Tying Instructions

HOOK: Partridge Captain Hamilton Nymph H1A, size 10/12.
THREAD: Light brown.
BODY: Pheasant tail fibres.
LEGS: Six pheasant tail fibres knotted twice.
WING: Red cock hackle points.
HACKLE: Ginger.

After laying down a bed of tying thread catch in three pheasant tail fibres by their tips at the hook bend. Now, by winding these fibres around the shank, form a skinny body that occupies approximately two-thirds of the total length, and tie off. So far· so good – now for the difficult bit. Take a further half dozen pheasant tail fibres and knot each of them twice. These knots represent leg joints. Once knotted, tie them carefully on the underside of the body so that they trail backwards. The idea of tying this pattern with trailing legs was conceived by the late Richard Walker who believed, and rightly so, that it was far more likely to catch than an artificial with legs fixed more realistically. The wings too should be tied trailing. Take your matched cock hackle points and fix them so they angle backwards at about forty-five degrees from the body. All that's left to do now is a good, long ginger hackle and a neatly finished head. Not the easiest of patterns to tie but well worth the effort.

THINGS TO REMEMBER
❦ SEPTEMBER ❦

Water temperature   Beginning to fall again.

Fly hatches   Although there is sometimes a last minute rush of activity from some species of aquatic insects the general hatching trend continues downwards. Subsequently terrestrial flies take on a greater importance to both fish and angler, especially those like the crane fly that appear in great numbers.

Fish behaviour   The declining supply of natural food should encourage the fish to begin feeding more boldly. It will also incite them to search vigorously for alternative food sources such as fish fry. Small fish will make up a large part of the trout's diet during this period.

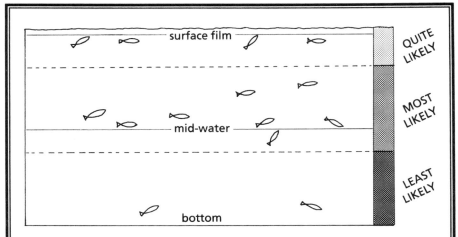

Fish Depth Guide – September

Fly selection September is *the* month for capturing fry feeding trout. My own 'No Name' lure (size 8/10) is an excellent fry pattern and won't let you down should you decide to give it a try. The Crane Fly (size 10/12) is another imitation that should be kept handy now that autumn has arrived. A large (size 12) Standard Nymph is a good general pattern for surface fishing this month.

Retrieve When casting to fry feeding trout the No Name lure should be retrieved with a series of short, sharp pulls, followed by a brief pause that allows the fly to sink. A brisk but irregular figure of eight can also be effective. The Crane Fly should be left for a short while after the cast has been made, then retrieved just sub-surface with long pulls.

Conditions on the day September is the second major change point of the year, and that change should be for the better! Bright sunshine during the early part of the month could still make things difficult for anglers but as autumn proper sets in and temperatures begin to fall the fishing should improve. Best conditions will still be overcast skies and enough wind to promote a vigorous ripple.

OCTOBER

GENERAL ADVICE

Way back at the very beginning of this book I realized that I'd have problems when I reached October. Of all the months of the year none are likely to produce the extremes of weather we may have to face during the next four weeks. It is very much a 'curate's egg' of a month, good in parts! The trouble is that the good days are *so* good, so utterly captivating, they can remain etched upon the mind and cloud our thinking so that when we try to recall the October weather from previous years we remember only golden Indian summers that seemed to go on forever, or sparkling frosty mornings as clear and cold as diamonds. These 'good days' even have a perfume all of their own – woodsmoke and falling leaves, apples, red and russet, slowly maturing on wooden shelves in cupboards that smell like wine.

Oh yes, October can be quite breathtaking. But there is another, more malevolent side to this month that we simply cannot ignore.

Sharply falling temperatures cause great masses of air to begin moving in massive turbulence, generating a force and power almost beyond human comprehension. Gales at this time of year are always violent and sometimes devastating. Ask anyone from the southern counties who experienced the great storm of 1987, they'll soon tell you. It was certainly brought home to me when I visited Bayham Lake down in Kent a few weeks after the event. The damage inflicted on mature woodland in that area was appalling. Even the few mighty oaks left upright stood witness to the ferocity of a wind that had taken them by their canopies and attempted to pluck them vertically from the ground, roots, soil and all. They now perch on what appear to be little circular islands of earth that stand two or three feet higher than the surrounding land.

So there, in a nutshell, is the problem. October is neither fish nor fowl, neither summer nor winter, and we will need to adopt a very flexible approach to our fishing if we are to be successful throughout this period.

Let's begin by looking at what we can expect conditions to be like if the month runs true to form and, for the time being at least, give the possibility of storms low priority in our thinking.

Conditions

Early October is often quite mild, though you'll probably notice a distinct nip in the air as evening approaches, and even if the day has been warm enough for shirt-sleeve fishing a good warm sweater will be needed if you intend staying on late. Mind you, there's not much to be gained by arriving at the waterside too early, or indeed staying on to fish after sunset. Most of the insect activity will occur in brief spells throughout the warmer hours of the day. As a consequence fish activity will, in general, be confined to those same brief periods. As the month progresses and the days grow shorter we can expect to see the first real frosts of the winter. These will, unfortunately, quickly chill the surface layers of the water, further discouraging fly hatches.

All this is beginning to sound a bit end of seasonish, so let's press on and look at the fishing itself. Believe me, there are lots of pluses to consider this month, not least the behaviour of our quarry, the trout.

Fish Behaviour

There is one thing we can be certain of at this time of year: the fish we are casting to will be very hungry. The quantity of natural food available in October is nowhere near sufficient to support the number of fish still existing in most of our still waters. It is hardly surprising therefore that any small hatch of fly is likely to provoke an immediate response from the trout. There will, of course, be quite lengthy periods when the fish do not show at all, though this won't necessarily mean that they are inactive. The pangs of hunger will drive them to search for sustenance and any angler contacting a shoal under these circumstances will enjoy some tremendous sport. But be aware, these fish will not stay in one place for long. To keep in touch with them you'll need to be light on your feet.

Surface activity will decrease steadily as November draws near until, finally, it is restricted to just the middle hours of the day, from approximately 11 a.m. until 3 p.m. Even then the activity will be sporadic rather than regular. Nevertheless, these brief rises should not be allowed to go to waste for they are a perfect example of that old adage, 'Good things come in small quantities'. Finding fish feeding on the top in late autumn is like discovering gold. Their willingness to come to the fly needs to be experienced to be truly appreciated. It is the sort of 'classic' surface fishing you dream about in early summer, the main difference being that October fish are likely to take the fly even more boldly.

But now, before euphoria gets the better of us, a word of warning. At some time this month you may find yourself casting unsuccessfully to rainbows that are shoaled even tighter than usual. They will probably have given away their position by milling about unhappily just below the surface. These will almost certainly be fish attempting to spawn. The shoal is usually made up of a couple of large, dark cock fish surrounded by a number of hens. The females struggle to get close enough to rub themselves against the males, hence the tightness of the shoal. Sadly, these pathetic efforts to procreate are doomed to failure for rainbows require a supply of clean running water to spawn properly. There is no doubt that some anglers find these fish a tempting target but I must be honest and say that I find the whole thing rather sad. I prefer to leave them in peace and would hope you will do the same. Anyway they're usually too preoccupied to come easily to the fly.

And finally, a few words about our native brown trout. In some parts of the country the brown trout season extends to the last day of October. In others the end date is somewhat earlier. I'd like first of all to offer a little advice and then follow that by asking a favour. The advice is that you check with your local authority regarding the 'close season' date for brown trout. This should be done before you start fishing. The last thing any of us need is the embarrassment of arriving back at the lodge and discovering we've killed an out-of-season fish. And now for the favour. If you hook and land a brownie that is clearly close to spawning then please return it *carefully* to the water even if the rules state that it can be killed and kept. Brown trout are expensive, too expensive to stock say some fishery owners, and in many cases stocking policies are drifting towards one hundred per cent rainbows. Any small contribution we anglers can make towards redressing that balance must be a good thing.

Tactics

Success in October depends very much on being in the right place at the right time. If you are the kind of angler who arrives at his local water and makes straight for one of the well known 'hot spots', determined to stick it out all day and hoping that the fish will decide to feed at some time or another, then you're likely to miss out on a lot of good sport. You'd be far better employed taking the search to the trout rather than waiting for them to come to you. That's what bank fishing is all about, being a bit of a gypsy, a wanderer. Half the thrill comes from finding the fish, the other half from persuading them to take the fly.

My strategy for October is to have two rods set up, one carrying a floating line and a large Olive nymph, the other holding a slow sinker with a lure of some sort on the point. If the weather is cold I will spend much of my time trying the deeper spots with the sinking line, all the time keeping an eye peeled for surface activity. It is a comforting thought that even on the coldest days one or two rainbows will still break the surface and by doing so betray the rest of the shoal to the man who has his wits about him. If I come across a rise of fish, no matter how brief, I am able to take full advantage by simply putting down one rod and picking up the other. If, on the other hand, I take a fish on the sinking line, I will persevere in that place for a while, working on the principle that where there is one rainbow there are likely to be others.

When fishing a sinking line it is vital that you know exactly the depth at which you first made contact with the fish so that you can repeat the cast over and over again. The only way to accomplish this is to begin counting as soon as the fly hits the water, slowly and regularly, like a metronome. Then, when the critical number is reached, begin your retrieve. If you find that after taking a couple of fish sport begins to slow, don't give up and move on right away. Try a change of depth, or a few casts either side of your position. As I said earlier these shoals tend to be very mobile and it could simply be that they've drifted further along the bank.

Should you be lucky enough to spot fish rising within casting range of the shore then don't hang about. Get to them as fast as you can. Knowing that surface activity in October is likely to be short lived makes fishing as much a test of nerve as of skill. If you start by making silly mistakes things have a habit of going from bad to worse. You'll find yourself stepping on your line halfway through a cast, or wrapping your leader around the topmost branches of that tree just ten yards behind you – yes, you should have noticed it before you began fishing. Then the fly becomes inextricably fixed in the sleeve of that jumper your wife

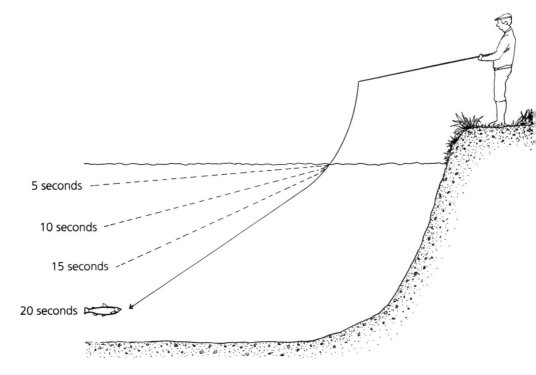

5 seconds

10 seconds

15 seconds

20 seconds

Angler counting to establish depth at which his fly is taken.

knitted so lovingly for you last Christmas. You'd like to cut it out but know that a hole the size of a tennis ball will take some explaining. Oh yes, all these things have happened to me at some time in the past.

So, begin as you mean to go on. Take a couple of deep breaths to steady your nerves, then commence. Make your casting quick and accurate. Lay the line nice and straight on the water, making sure there is no slack between you and the fly that might disguise the sharp pull of a fish taking 'on the drop'. If the trout intends having the fly it will usually be in the first couple of yards of the retrieve so be prepared. With luck, and a steady hand, you could well have five or six fish on the bank before the rise is over and that's a wonderful feeling, knowing you were up to the job. But if you make a mess of things don't be too upset. There's always a next time.

Although those of you with only one rod will be at something of a disadvantage there are certain steps you can take to minimize this, one of them being your choice of line. I would suggest you go for the slowest sinking line possible. An intermediate is better than one that sinks too fast. When fishing deep you will need a fairly long leader, up to twenty feet if the bank-side vegetation allows and you can manage to cast that sort of length. On the point mount a lure with plenty of lead built in so

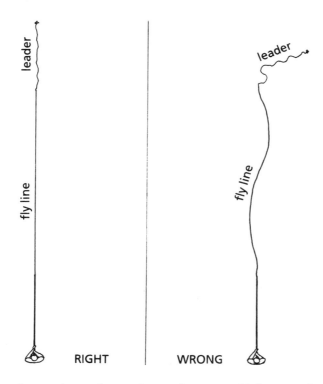

Lay the line down nice and straight on the water. Make sure there is no slack between you and your fly.

that it sinks quickly. Too light a fly will mean you spending most of your time waiting for it to reach the required depth rather than fishing. And do de-grease the leader thoroughly so that it doesn't hinder the fly's downward progress. There you are, ready to go.

But what if you suddenly come across that rise we spoke of earlier? Simply change to a light fly, a sixty second job at the outside, then begin casting to the fish as you would normally do with a floating line, retrieving as soon as the fly disappears beneath the surface. If your line really is a slow sinker the fly should remain in the upper water layers long enough to be effective.

There's just one other thing worth mentioning before we leave the subject of tactics altogether – trout will still be harrying those shoals of coarse fry this month so keep in mind September's advice for dealing with the fry feeders.

TWO FLIES FOR OCTOBER

For the traditional trout angler October must be the saddest month of the year, heralding as it does the end of the fly fishing season proper. But now is not the time to allow the negative aspects of this month to overtake us. Let's concentrate instead on the positive side of things. For instance, what flies should we be considering if we intend to go out in a blaze of glory? Well here's the good news: I have saved one of the best until last. The fly I'm about to recommend is an all-time favourite of mine, a pattern I have used successfully for a number of years and one that has caught fish from waters the length and breadth of the country. It is a Dark Olive Nymph, made from seal's fur, simple to tie and even simpler to use. A real fisherman's fly.

The Dark Olive Nymph

At first glance there is nothing at all remarkable about this artificial, especially when dry. But tie it to a piece of nylon, dunk it in water and jig it up and down for half a minute, then look at it again. Those seal's fur fibres have been teased out by the action of the water and are now the most lifelike of insect limbs. The transformation is quite magical. But here's the rub. I haven't yet found an alternative to seal's fur that will give this almost perfect effect. Certainly there are some admirable materials on the market nowadays that will satisfy most tasks in fly tying, but none of them quite measure up to seal's fur for this particular pattern.

Just lately I've been reduced to scouring tackle shops countrywide for the odd packet. The colour at the time of purchase doesn't worry me. I'm happy to dye it myself. I can only hope that before my steadily dwindling supply is completely exhausted someone will come up with an alternative material that has truly similar characteristics to those of seal's fur.

How to Fish It

This Nymph is a 'top of the water' fly, tied specifically to deal with fish that are feeding or searching for food in the upper water layers. It should be fished on a floating or intermediate line in conjunction with a leader of at least fifteen feet and a point of 4 lb breaking strain.

If this seems to be a little light then let me offer you a word of advice. In ninety per cent of the cases where anglers suffer line breakages, the damage occurs on the strike. This usually happens for one of the following reasons:

1. The leader has been kinked or frayed while fishing and the angler hasn't noticed.

2. The fish takes the fly at speed and simply cracks off a section of leader.

3. The angler is striking too enthusiastically.

Of the three the last is probably the most common. Experienced anglers, especially when fishing a floating line, realize that a smart lifting of the rod is usually enough to ensure a solid hook hold. If you've suffered a few breakages recently why not give it a try? Nothing ventured nothing gained. Now back to the fishing.

Once you have located your quarry and the cast has been made, wait a couple of seconds to allow the nymph to sink a few inches, then begin a gentle figure of eight retrieve. Offers should come early rather than late and be very positive.

Tying Instructions

HOOK: Partridge Captain Hamilton Nymph H1A, size 10/12.
THREAD: Green.
BODY AND THORAX: Dark olive seal's fur.
RIB: Copper wire.
WING CASE: Goose wing.

As promised this really is one of the easiest patterns to tie. Begin as usual with a neat bed of tying thread and just enough lead to help the fly turn over on the cast. Tie this in firmly and return the thread to the bend of the hook, catching in the wire rib as you go. Now dub on your seal's fur and build up the body, making it slightly plump. Follow this with the rib. The wing case I use is a slip cut from the wing feather of a Canada goose. The fibres are a dull grey on the top and quite shiny underneath. Fix the slip so that the dull side will be on show when tying is complete. Now dub on the thorax, (slightly fatter than the body) and finish tying in the wing case. Oh, and most important, don't forget to pick out a few fibres from the body and thorax of the fly with a needle. This will give you that straggly look we talked about earlier.

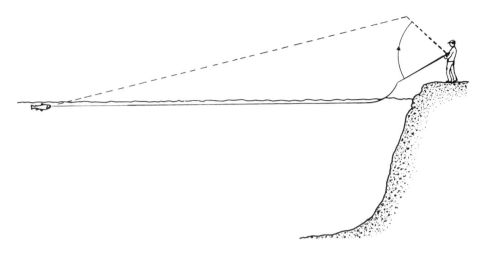

Experienced anglers, especially when fishing a floating line, realize that a smart lifting of the rod is usually enough to ensure a solid hook hold.

The Montana Nymph

There are a great many anglers who would rather be found in bed with the wife (or husband) of their best friend rather than be caught fishing a lure! Their reasons? It's usually a simple case of prejudice. Let's be honest, we fly fishers can be as narrow-minded and bigoted as the rest, even more so on occasions.

There are, however, some who simply prefer the gentler, more contemplative style of fishing that goes with the use of nymphs and natural imitations and it is for these people that I have chosen this last fly in my book. It complements in almost every way the Dark Olive Nymph we have just finished discussing. I described that as a 'top of the water' fly. The Montana, on the other hand, is very much a pattern for fishing deep and is an excellent alternative to the lure when it comes to the business of trying to locate fish when there are no visible signs to help you. As far as I know it was tied originally as a stonefly or bottom creeper of some kind, and although many anglers seem happy to use it as a standard nymph pattern these days I still believe it to be at its best when used on or near the lake bed.

How to Fish It

There will come a time in the colder months ahead when you will be faced with an expanse of cold, grey, apparently lifeless water. You will work hard trying to find the fish, walk great distances and search diligently, and receive absolutely no help at all from the trout who will be lying low. 'What should we do at times like that?' is a question I'm often asked. The truth of the matter is that there is little any of us can do except to use what knowledge we have to locate the known fish holding areas that exist at all fisheries, and of course rely upon that 'gut feel' or sixth sense that tells us when we are in the vicinity of fish. Mind you, it's important also to be using a fly in which you have a measure of confidence, one that you are sure will be acceptable to the trout more often than not, and that is the strength of the Montana. It has a happy knack of generating offers when many other patterns will fail.

A slow sinking line, a leader of around twelve feet and a point of 4 lb breaking strain is the set up I favour for this 'deep search' type of fishing.

Once I have selected the area in which I intend to concentrate my efforts I make up my mind to fish it thoroughly, no half measures. A fair sized shoal of rainbows need occupy no more space than three square yards and can easily be missed. In order not to do so I find it necessary to adopt a slightly mechanical approach that sees me making my first cast directly out into the pool, followed by fan casts on either side. If no offers are forthcoming I move along the bank a little and repeat the procedure.

I give the fly plenty of time to get somewhere near the bottom before starting the retrieve and, during its descent, keep an eagle eye on that foot of line at the rod tip for any sudden movement that might signify a fish intercepting it on the way down.

Tying Instructions

HOOK: Partridge Captain Hamilton Nymph H1A, size 10.
THREAD: Black.
TAIL: Two black hackle tips tied in a 'V'.
BODY: Black seal's fur substitute.
THORAX: Yellow Antron body wool.
WING CASE: Goose.
HACKLE: Black hen.

The original Montana Nymph used chenille for the body and thorax but it is a material I have never particularly liked and so I have substituted an alternative. I should stress, however, that this is very much a personal choice.

Wind on a layer of thread along the shank of the hook from eye to bend before tying in plenty of lead. The amount of lead used should only be limited by the body profile. Remember, we don't want to lose that nymphal shape.

When this part of the operation is complete return the thread once more to the bend and tie in the two black hackle tips, 'V' formation. Then dub on the seal's fur substitute and begin building up the body of the fly, working back towards the eye of the hook. The wing case is once again a slip cut from a goose feather but this time it is fixed so that the shiny side is uppermost when finished. Now for the final stages. Tie in a little yellow body wool, not too much, and form a slender thorax. Follow this with a sparse hackle and finish by laying the wing case in position and tying off.

THINGS TO REMEMBER
ᒡᔪ OCTOBER ᒡᔪ

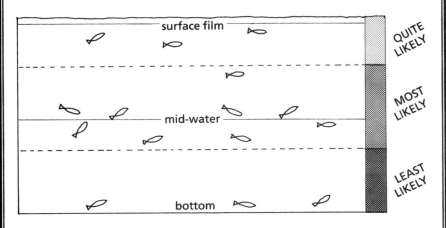

Fish Depth Guide – October

Water temperature Cooling rapidly.

Fly hatches Heavy fly hatches are now a thing of the past. There is still an outside chance of a sparse hatch of some kind on a warm afternoon early in the month but generally the cycle of insect reproduction is over for the year.

Fish behaviour Trout should now be feeling the pangs of hunger and, given the opportunity, will usually come quite boldly to anglers' flies. As the month progresses peak feeding times will shift gradually towards the warmer, middle hours of the day. The fish will continue to search the upper water layers for food, but with the arrival of the first frost of the year surface activity will decrease.

Fly selection The Dark Olive Nymph (size 10) recommended for this month is a brilliant general purpose pattern for fishing in the upper water layers. It is not tied to represent any particular species of insect but that doesn't stop it being extremely effective under the right conditions.

The Montana Nymph (size 10) combines the two colours of black and green that always seem to do well early and late in the season. This is another excellent nymph pattern that I prefer to fish deep.

Retrieve For both the Montana and the Dark Olive Nymph my chosen retrieve would be a gentle figure of eight.

Conditions on the day The sun in October loses its harsh edge and is unlikely to upset the trout. Indeed late, warm sunshine can be a positive benefit in as much as it inhibits the cooling of the water surface. A sudden, heavy frost, on the other hand, can depress sport like nothing else. Best conditions will be warm, calm days with some sunshine.

WINTER FISHING

GENERAL ADVICE

Fly fishing for rainbow trout during the winter months is still very much in its infancy and has yet to adopt a form we can all recognize or patterns we can rely upon. Having said that, there is one issue on which we are left in no doubt. The traditionalists are totally against the pursuit of trout between the months of October and April. I, on the other hand, see nothing wrong with it at all, providing that the fish I'm catching are clean and bright, that is. Now the last thing I want to do is to get involved in some high-blown moral or ethical argument on the rights and wrongs of winter fishing. Our chosen sport is already under enough pressure from outside groups without us arguing amongst ourselves, so let's just agree to live and let live, shall we? If you're one of those people who believe that rods and reels should be packed away on October 31st, then close the book at this point and read no further. I will assume that those of you who are still with me are interested in taking advantage of this extension to the old season. In which case I can promise you some really splendid sport. All we need to do is to exercise a little discretion with regard to the weather.

Mild Spells

Because of Britain's geographical position our climate is, on the whole, temperate, though changeable. Winters are generally benign when compared with much of Europe and although there are almost always three or four weeks of intense cold there are also prolonged periods of mild weather when temperatures remain comparatively high. I have found these conditions to be as good as any for winter fishing and tend to put in as many trips as possible during these warmer spells. If you decide to do the same you can expect to see a few small flies hatching on the drier days and a subsequent amount of fish activity on or near the surface.

Low Temperatures

During the bitter winter of 1986/87 I caught fish in temperatures as low as minus eleven! If nothing else this proved to me that trout cope very well with cold weather. The thing that will upset them is a sudden and dramatic fall in temperature. So if you're in the mood for a day out at your local fishery, avoid the sudden cold snap. You'd be far better off sitting tight for a few days, even if the weather remains cold. Give the fish a little time to acclimatize.

If the temperature falls well below freezing it makes sense to ring the fishery beforehand rather than turning up on the day and finding ice two inches thick stretching from one bank to the other. Remember also that still water tends to ice up first around its perimeter, affecting the bank angler before the boat man. And while I'm thinking about it let me give you a tip. Even when the thermometer plunges well below zero and most of the fisheries in your area are frozen over, there are still likely to be the odd lucky few that will remain fishable. These won't be, as you might expect, those that occupy the most sheltered positions, but are more often than not those in the windiest, most exposed situations where the wind keeps the water moving. It is this movement that inhibits freezing. If you have difficulty in accepting this then take a look at any large, open stretch of water near you this winter. The windiest spots will always be the last to ice over.

Snow

I don't mind in the least fishing with snow on the ground, even if the fall has been heavy. Fresh falls of snow don't harm the fishing too much, at least that's been my experience. It's only after the weather warms up and a thaw takes place that the angler's problems begin. Nothing kills sport as quickly as snow broth running into rivers, lakes and reservoirs, ice cold and de-oxygenated. My advice would be to forget fishing for a short time after a thaw has taken place, even though you might be tempted by the rise in temperature.

Rain

Under normal circumstances rain during the winter indicates that the weather is warming up and if that's the case then I'll willingly risk a wetting on the off-chance of catching a few fish. Unfortunately there are also those times when the wind comes from the north-east, bringing with it a fine, bitterly cold rain that falls like a grey curtain across the landscape, numbing fingers and cheeks and finding its way past collars and cuffs. I honestly feel that this is the worst kind of weather in which to fish – not only is it uncomfortable, it's unproductive too for the trout seem to dislike it as much as I do. Anyway, when conditions are like this I don't shift from my fireside.

Value for Money

Let me now tell you what I expect for my money when I go winter fishing. First I like to know that the waters I visit have a policy of introducing fresh fish at frequent intervals and by frequent I mean at least on a weekly basis. The thing to keep in mind is that rainbows lose condition very soon after stocking and although many fisheries tend to stock a high percentage of hen fish (they maintain condition longer than the cocks) they too will darken after a period of time in the wild. Putting it quite simply, the sooner the fish are caught the better their condition will be. An increasing number of fisheries are beginning to stock with triploid (sexless) trout that don't experience the spawning agony. This seems an ideal solution to the problem of winter stocking although, inevitably, the extra cost of raising such creatures will be reflected in increased fishing charges.

Another idea that appeals to me is the reduced winter charge for a reduced fish limit. For example, if the normal cost of a day ticket is £20 for an eight fish limit, then the winter charge could be £12 for four fish. This seems fair enough, particularly when I think of those extremely cold days in January and February when only the four middle hours of the day are worth fishing.

Winter Tactics

To describe tactics for winter fishing really won't take long. We will be fishing essentially for fresh stockies and, as usual, our biggest problem will be in finding them. Once found they should not be too difficult to catch for they're bound to be extremely hungry. Don't forget there's very little natural food in the larder at this time of year. Any of the usual fly patterns will take rainbows providing they're fished half well. But, at the risk of repeating myself, there will be days when finding the fish will be like searching for a needle in a haystack. All we can do then is to search and move, search and move, all the time keeping watch for the odd fish that rolls near the surface, betraying the position of the shoal.

Alright, that's enough theory for a while. I'd like to round things off now by asking you to read on and join me on a day's winter fishing that took place during December, almost five years ago.

MID-WINTER AND WET FEET

I was late arriving as usual. Not that I was worried. There had been another heavy frost during the night and I didn't expect to see much action before midday. Nevertheless I'd promised to meet Dave at 8.30 and it was already 9.15. Guiltily I parked my car alongside his in the car park. Although the sun was bright overhead there was no warmth in it and Dave's windscreen was already whitening under a fresh coating of frost. I tackled up quickly and set off down the path to the pool.

Finding Dave wasn't going to be a problem. This was a small fishery, no more than forty acres, and roughly rectangular in shape. The banks were fairly flat and there really was nowhere for an angler to tuck himself away out of sight, not even someone like my friend who knew this particular water like the back of his hand.

He looked perished as I crunched across the grass to where he was sitting. He'd found a bench and was drinking tea, steaming hot, from a cup clasped in both hands. Dave always arrived at the venue earlier than I did and usually profited from doing so. Not today though.

'Caught them all?' I greeted him cheerfully.

'Not so much as an offer,' he grumbled, 'and I've been at it for over an hour.'

I sat with him and listened while he recounted the events of the morning so far. That didn't take long. He'd settled in the spot where he'd seen a single fish roll and, quite rightly, decided to stick it out there until I arrived. Unfortunately it meant fishing into a steady breeze that came straight across the pool from the north and all he'd got for his efforts were eyes that watered and cheeks tinged purple by the cold. After a minute or two the hot tea began to buck him up and he became much more animated as he told me about a successful session at this same fishery just two days earlier.

'All along this bank,' he traced the margins with his finger, 'there were fish rising all along here.'

I didn't fancy bashing a short line out into that wind but, as usual, Dave's enthusiasm was infectious and I found myself twenty yards to his right, fingers and nose numbed by the cold, throwing a leaded nymph into the grey, choppy water that broke in tiny wavelets at my feet. A strong breeze can be chilly even on a summer's day, but in the third week of December it was plain torture.

We stuck at it for another hour, sixty minutes of cast and retrieve, the monotony relieved only by the appearance of a young swan still dressed in his pale brown suit of juvenile feathers. He trod water in front of Dave, glaring hopefully at my friend's lunchbox. As the time passed the other side of the pool began to look more and more attractive to me. Trees offered some shelter from the wind even though they were stark and almost leafless. Wooden fishing stages had been built for anglers, interconnected by a wooden walkway, and an inviting band of calm water some fifteen yards wide lay just in front of them. 'Let's split up and try the far side,' I suggested hopefully. Dave didn't need much persuading. It would certainly be more comfortable with the wind on our backs and could hardly be less productive than our present position.

The sharp walk around the pool helped us warm up and by the time we reached the fishing stages our spirits, like our body temperatures, were rising. Dave stopped at the first spot, declaring his intention to work his way methodically along that stretch of bank. I pressed on quite some distance until I reached a deep reed bed some fifty yards from the bottom end of the pool. It was here, where the walkway ended and the jungle of brittle white stalks began, that I saw a fish move, the only one

I'd seen that morning. It rolled tight in alongside the reed bed, halfway between where I stood and the corner of the pool. I leaned out over the water as far as I dared for a better look, just in time to see a second fish bulge under the surface very close to where the first had risen. It was quite impossible to reach them with a cast from where I stood. The fishing platforms had been designed to allow the angler to throw his line directly out into the pool, not parallel with the bank, and a large bush just four yards to my right made even a sideways flick out of the question. Somehow I'd have to get to the fish through the reed bed.

I retraced my steps along the walkway until I could reach the bank behind. Then, sticking to the dry ground, walked back through a thicket until I judged I was roughly at the centre point of the reeds. Happily my calculations proved accurate. I headed back down to the waterside, the ground underfoot becoming distinctly softer, and reached the reed bed at almost exactly the halfway point. I was a little surprised to find that someone had been there before me. A narrow channel had been cleared through the stalks, no more than three feet wide. I checked around for footprints but there were none, which suggested that the access channel had been made some time previously.

After hanging my bag on a nearby tree I slipped my priest into a handy pocket and, testing for depth with my landing net handle, began wading out, rod held above my head. Black mud billowed up from the bottom, releasing the usual foul stench of rotting vegetation. After just a few, faltering steps the water was up over my knees. I could feel its coldness through my thermal socks and 'long johns'. Two more steps and the level was within a couple of inches of my wader tops, yet I was still a good three feet away from open water. Well, if this was as far as I could go then so be it. I didn't intend to go to all this trouble and not wet a line.

I forced the landing net handle into the soft mud at my feet, then glanced over my shoulder at the tangle of bushes only ten yards behind. Intimidating but not impossible. Unhooking the Nymph from the keeper ring near the rod butt, I pulled off a few yards of line. The fish I'd seen had been rising close in and even allowing for the disturbance I'd made wading I still expected to reach them with a modest cast. I flicked the rod forward, dropping the fly and some line onto open water. Then, checking once more behind me, gauging the distance to the bushes, I hauled and punched the rod through the gap in the reeds, shooting as much of the spare line as possible after it. Fifteen yards out the Nymph splashed down. I straightened the line and watched the leader slowly disappear, pulled down by the weight of the fly. I'd made up my mind to start fishing deep as no other fish had shown since those first two. Using a floating line, as I do for much of the time, has taught me to give the fly plenty of time to hit bottom, which in this case I estimated to be about eight feet. I began a slow count of thirty, thinking to myself that if I didn't begin catching fairly quickly then I'd work my way up through the water levels in the hope of contacting the fish nearer the surface.

'Twenty-eight, twenty-nine, thirty.' The last tumbler clicked into place and I began the retrieve.

During that first twenty minutes three stockies took my fly as I dragged it in a slow, pull and pause, routine across the lake bed. Each time there was nothing I could do but hang on, not giving an inch, and each time they came flashing furiously to the surface, all cartwheels and bristling fins. Any onlooker would have thought it a most brutal and clumsy way of playing the fish but stuck where I was, three feet back in the reeds, I was left with no choice. One of the problems with hooking fish and holding on tight is that, inevitably, you will suffer losses. Mine occurred when the last of the three stockies began tailwalking, finally throwing the hook. Shortly after that all activity ceased.

An uneventful half hour followed and I was about to move on when my fly was taken again, very gently. As soon as I tightened up I realized I was into the best fish of the day so far. It fought sensibly in the deep water, pulling the rod tip down almost level with the surface and making the line whistle. I simply hung on and prayed. It was a full two minutes before he began to weaken and I allowed myself the luxury of contemplating victory. He'd done his worst, running and boring hard both right and left, only to have his head pulled around each time by the power of the rod. And now he was on his way up.

I groped for the net and slid it forward, resting it on the flattened reeds just below the surface. Perhaps it was the realization that he was almost on the top that gave him the energy to make one last desperate dash for freedom. He bolted straight at me, swerving to the right at the last minute and burying his head and shoulders in the reed bed. Everything went solid and I cursed under my breath, but kept the line tight. The battle wasn't lost yet. I could see the trout's tail sticking out of the reeds, waving gently a foot or two down. One handed I turned the landing net around and poked the handle down into the water in the general direction of the fish's nose. It worked! He engaged reverse gear and backed out of his hidey hole.

Under the pressure of the rod the trout came to the surface, rolling slowly onto his side. He was finished. It was a cock fish but in stunningly good condition. I swung the net the right way around and reached for him.

'He'll go over three pounds.' The words were still on my lips when the fly pulled out. The fish lay there, just a foot away from the edge of my landing net, too exhausted to realize it was free. I panicked and took a step forward, lunging at him. Half in and half out of the net he finally woke up, flapped that big square tail, and was gone!

It was then I noticed my wader filling up with water. I backed up quickly, but too late. It was already over my ankle and the trouser leg was acting like blotting paper.

My disappointment was a physical thing. I returned to dry land feeling stiff and cold. The sound of twigs breaking underfoot heralded Dave's arrival. He'd apparently been searching for me for some time. We sat in silence while I emptied two pints of water from my wader, then wrung another pint from my sock. It was a further minute before I was able to describe the loss of the fish and my subsequent wetting. 'I should have warned you,' he said. 'That little channel is too deep to fish properly in the winter. In fact you did well to get anything out of there. I still can't see how you managed it.' That made me feel a little better. As we talked and I drank my coffee the day seemed to grow a little warmer, though the wisps of steam curling from my cup belied that impression. I fancy the warmth I felt was that of companionship for, as someone much wiser than I once said, 'To fish alone is better than not to fish at all, but to fish in good company adds infinitely to the pleasure.'

After lunch we circumnavigated the pool again, adopting our usual tactics of search and move, until we stumbled across a shoal of fish feeding hard on a hatch of tiny, brown, smut-like flies that we couldn't identify. Then, with teams of small Buzzers, we completed our limits with such ease that it made a mockery of my earlier strenuous efforts. Yet it would be the two fish I landed, and those others lost amongst the reeds, that stayed longest in my mind. But then don't we always value most highly those things for which we have worked hardest?

It was almost dark when, at 3.30, I said goodbye to my friend and drove out of the car park. The temperature had dropped alarmingly in the past hour and my headlights picked out leafless shrubs at the roadside, gleaming white with a fresh dusting of frost. My trouser leg still felt damp and uncomfortable against my skin. Ah well, these things happen. All in all it had been a most enjoyable outing, the sort of day that would help me endure those cold and icy weeks still to come, when fishing might be impossible and all I'd have to live on would be the memory of a day in mid winter . . . and wet feet!

TWO FLIES FOR WINTER

The Tadpole

As the year draws to a close and the bitter months of winter arrive, fly selection once again takes on a slightly less important role for the angler. As long as patterns are on the large side and have plenty of movement when drawn through the water they will catch trout. The size is important because winter fish are usually very hungry indeed and find a large mouthful particularly attractive. And on those cold days when the fish are reluctant in the extreme to do anything but sulk on or near the bottom, it needs a pattern with plenty of life in it to provoke a response.

Two things must be said about the Tadpole range of flies. In the first place there are few creations more mobile. And in the second, although they may not be the most elegant pattern to have ever been invented, they most certainly do catch fish. In fact since their introduction they have been the subject of some controversy, many of the more traditional fly fishers believing that they make fishing too easy! They contend that flies of this kind allow the less skilled anglers to capture a higher percentage of fish, thus dissuading them from developing their talents further with some of the more traditional patterns.

I'm pleased to say that I don't have any hang-ups of that kind. Quite the opposite. I love to see people catching fish and, whenever possible, will go out of my way to offer any help I can. And, providing they stay within the rules of the sport, I don't really care what flies they might be using. That is why I'm quite happy to commend to you my own version of the Tadpole for use in the colder months ahead.

How to Fish It

During the winter I would suggest you fish these Tadpole patterns on intermediate or slow sinking lines. It is true to say that on the odd occasion, when covering very deep water from dam walls and other similar situations, you might find the need for a medium or fast sinker. But this will prove to be the exception rather than the rule. More often than not the depth of water you'll be casting into from the bank will be fifteen feet or less, in which case a slow sinking line is adequate.

Winter tactics are fairly unsophisticated when compared with summer fishing. A leader of twelve to fifteen feet terminating in a point of 5 lb breaking strain will be fine for most occasions. The Tadpole should be fished as a single fly (the addition of droppers, particularly on windy days, is more trouble than it is worth at this time of year) and the fly should be soaked well before fishing commences. This is particularly important with marabou patterns as the feather has an infuriating habit of retaining air unless it is squeezed out. Try fishing it without a proper soaking and you'll see what I mean. Those soft fibres only begin their seductive pulsing and wriggling through the water when thoroughly wet.

The retrieve I favour most times with Tadpole patterns is an interrupted figure of eight. By that I mean an irregular, fast and slow, twitchy action designed to produce maximum movement from the fly.

By the way, make a point of checking at the end of each retrieve that the marabou tail has not wound itself around the bend of the hook. This happens regularly in breezy conditions and is easily missed unless you know what to look for. It may seem only a minor detail but believe me, unless that tail is fully extended, the Tadpole has very little about it to attract the fish.

Tying Instructions

HOOK: Partridge Streamer D3ST, size 10/12.
THREAD: Black/white.
TAIL AND BODY: Marabou feather, black or white.
THORAX: Seal's fur substitute, black/white/lime green.
RIB: Broad silver tinsel.
HACKLE: Soft hen.

After putting down the usual layer of thread along the hook shank, tie in your lead before returning the thread to the hook bend. Now fix a plump marabou tail that overhangs the hook bend by approximately one inch and, while you're at it, catch in the rib. When this is done take a second pinch of marabou and tie it in by its tips. (This is to be the body material.) Then, after returning the thread to the eye of the hook, twist the feather fibres into a loose rope and proceed to wind this on, building up a fluffy body. Tie off two thirds of the way along the hook shank and overlay with the broad silver rib. When the rib is fixed in position dub on a slightly swelling thorax and finish off with a sparse hackle.

Tadpoles can be tied in a variety of colours (orange is a particular favourite with many anglers during the months of high summer) but I tend to stick in the main to black or white. On occasions, however, I do like to enhance the white version with a lime green thorax.

The Black and Peacock Spider

In recommending this traditional little pattern I have, for the first time, consciously allowed prejudice to influence me in my choice of fly. Perhaps I should have taken the easy way out and suggested yet another lure. Had I done so I'm pretty certain no one would have questioned that decision. After all, winter fishing and lures go together like Wimbledon and strawberries. At least that's how most people see it.

But tucked away in the recesses of my mind, like pearls inside a barnacled old oyster, are memories of those odd, gentle days we seem to get each winter when the bitter weather suddenly relents and temperatures climb unseasonably.

Then, before we know it, sparse hatches of tiny flies begin to appear, encouraging one or two fish to show on the surface. These are days stolen from springtime and knowing they won't last long makes me all the more determined to make the most of them. That is why I always carry a few Black and Peacock Spiders tucked away in a corner of my fly box. They are the perfect artificial for such conditions.

Sadly, many traditional patterns have fallen out of fashion over the past few years. These include the Black and Peacock Spider. On one occasion, merely to satisfy my own curiosity, I made a point of asking a number of anglers whether or not they had ever used this fly. The first seventeen didn't even carry the pattern and the eighteenth (who had two in his box) admitted having only tried them a couple of times, briefly! Ah well. Maybe these scant few words will help bring about a revival in the Black and Peacock's fortunes.

How to Fish It

For me the Black and Peacock has always produced its best results during the colder months of the year, let's say from late autumn through to late spring – that period when there is little natural insect activity and non-specific fly patterns come into their own. Although it has been used with some success to imitate the floating snails that abound at some fisheries, I don't believe it was tied with any particular creature in mind. Nevertheless it has a decidedly 'natural' look about it when wet.

I usually fish the Black and Peacock in typical Nymph fashion on a leader of around fifteen feet and to a point of 4 lb breaking strain. I do, however, prefer a slightly faster retrieve than I would normally employ when using Nymphs. This can sometimes be a problem if I want to keep the fly down a foot or so beneath the surface. The Black and Peacock is an unusually buoyant pattern and, when used in conjunction with a floating line, tends to rise in the water unless plenty of lead has been added during tying.

To overcome this 'lifting' problem I prefer most times to fish the fly on an intermediate line. This allows me to retrieve at any speed I like while maintaining the chosen depth.

Perhaps it would be a good idea at this point if I offered an explanation for my insistence on fishing surface flies slightly deeper during the winter months. I believe that, even when some fish appear to be feeding on the top, most of the activity is still taking place a foot or so further down. Winter fly hatches are inevitably sparse and with the trout competing for food the majority of insects will be picked off well before they reach the surface. I'm also quite positive that this situation is not unique to winter fishing. There are many fisheries that do not enjoy prolific hatches of fly even during the warmer months of the year. Local anglers at these venues soon cotton on to the fact that artificials presented on floating lines near the surface produce less fish than those offered on intermediate lines slightly deeper.

Tying Instructions

HOOK: Partridge Captain Hamilton L2A, size 10/12/14.
THREAD: Black.
BODY: Peacock herl.
HACKLE: Black hen.

There can be very few simpler patterns to tie than this. Simply begin as usual by laying down a nice, neat bed of tying thread along the hook shank from eye to bend and layer on a little lead for ballast. Tie this in and return the thread to the hook bend. Then select two plump strands of peacock herl and tie them in by their tips. When that has been done twist the two strands gently together. This should prevent them parting when you come to build up the body of the fly. Now begin forming a slightly fat body by winding the twisted herl around the hook shank, working back towards the eye. Tie off leaving just enough room for the hackle. And now a word of warning: try not to over-dress at this point. A bushy hackle just doesn't look right on this fly in my opinion. Two turns is quite enough. Finish off with a neat, nicely proportioned head and there you have it – a Black and Peacock Spider. Innocuous to look at but, under the right circumstances, a real wolf in sheep's clothing.

THINGS TO REMEMBER
ꙮ WINTER ꙮ

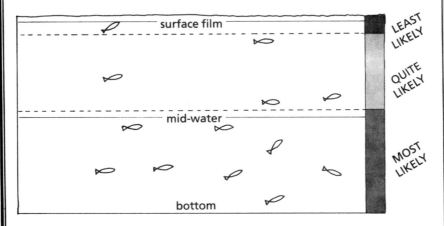

Fish Depth Guide – Winter

Water temperature   Extremely cold.

Fly hatches   Virtually nonexistent. There will be times when, on unseasonably warm days, a few tiny flies will begin hatching. Unfortunately these occasions are something of a rarity and cannot be depended upon.

Fish behaviour   Although extreme cold will drive the fish into deep water and discourage feeding, any slight rise in temperature could see them searching the mid to upper water levels actively for food. During these periods they will come most willingly to the angler's fly. Most feeding activity will now be confined to the middle hours of the day unless the weather is unseasonably warm.

Fly selection   The Tadpole (size 10/12) is an ideal pattern for the colder months, a fly with plenty of movement and just what's required on a dreary winter day. If we are lucky enough to get the odd mild spell between now and spring, the Black and Peacock Spider (sizes 10 to 14) could give you a day to remember.

Retrieve   For the Tadpole I would recommend an irregular or interrupted figure of eight. Don't forget to check before re-casting that the tail of the fly is not caught up around the hook bend. With the Black and Peacock Spider I have found a steady, slightly faster than usual, figure of eight to be most productive.

Conditions on the day   Trout will feed for brief periods in almost all winter conditions providing they have time to become acclimatized. Sudden sharp falls in temperature and heavy frosts tend to discourage fish activity, as does a rapid thaw after snow has fallen – at least that's been my experience. To my mind the best winter conditions will always be prolonged mild periods, but perhaps that's asking too much. And so I would advise you to simply wait until the weather settles into a pattern before venturing out.

FISHING THE
❧ DRY FLY ❧

GENERAL ADVICE

It is true to say that for every one fish I take on a dry fly I probably take ninety-nine others on a wet pattern of some kind. That seems quite an imbalance, I know, but when you consider that most aquatic insects spend ninety-nine per cent of their lives below the surface of the water you can see that my catch ratio of 99-1 is about right.

Looking at statistics like that, coldly and clinically, tends to lead one to the conclusion that dry fly fishing is a relatively unimportant tactic to the stillwater angler. But what was it the man said about 'Lies, damned lies and statistics'? It's one thing to weigh the odds logically – I'm all for that – but to make a calculated decision not to explore the advantages of the dry fly on the basis that it is a weapon rarely used and therefore not worth pursuing would be a serious mistake for any angler to make.

In this uncertain world there are few things we can rely upon, except perhaps the phenomenon known as 'Sod's Law'. You must have come across it at some time – in simple terms 'Sod's Law' dictates that if you are unprepared for any event then you can be absolutely certain that it *will* occur, and sooner rather than later. For example, I'd love to know how many anglers have gone off for a day's fishing only to find they've left their landing nets behind. It's happened to me in the past and I don't mind admitting it. Unfortunately I didn't realize my mistake until I was tackling up at the waterside. Having only two alternatives, to return home for my net (a car journey of almost an hour) or to take a chance and fish on, I chose the latter. I was helped in my decision by the knowledge that the fishery in question was not known as a big fish water, the average size of stockies being little more than a pound and a quarter. So how come that the first two fish I hooked (and lost while trying to beach them) were both in excess of five pounds? Sod's Law, that's how.

Many years ago I learned a vital lesson along the same lines with regard to dry fly fishing. I watched an elderly man on a warm, dull May morning taking fish on tiny pond olives while all around him other anglers were failing. If I close my eyes I can still see him now. He fished seated, crouched on an old basket that creaked like a galleon under full sail as he moved. He was casting his fly no more than ten yards, putting it down delicately on the edge of a patch of ripple. The wind would catch it, swinging it around like a tiny sail boat and pushing it into the broken water where the fish were waiting. There would be a splashy rise, a lazy lifting of the rod tip, and another trout was winkled out of the shoal.

That incident brought home the value of the dry fly to me. I wasn't one of those anglers fishing near the old man that day, though I've no doubt that if I had been I would have enjoyed no more success than they did. Like them I would have persevered with my Nymphs and wet flies, if for no other reason than the few dry flies I owned were poor moth-eaten things that were unlikely to fool even the most naive of trout. I was, quite frankly, unprepared. But I learned my lesson well. Nowadays you won't catch me out so easily.

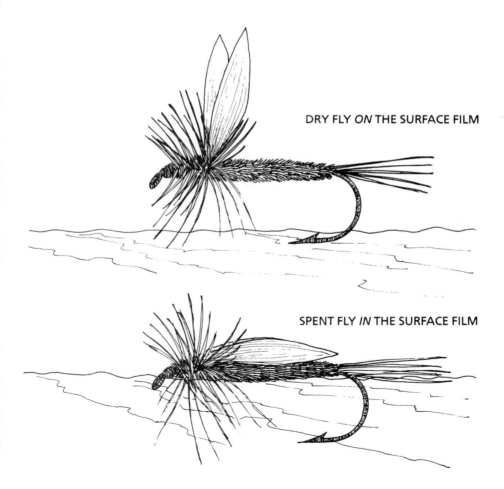

DRY FLY *ON* THE SURFACE FILM

SPENT FLY *IN* THE SURFACE FILM

It would make sense at this point to go on to discuss tactics for dry fly fishing, but before we do that I'd like first to define the expression 'dry fly' so that we're all sure exactly what the term means. A dry fly, as opposed to a wet fly, is designed to sit on top of the surface film (not in it) and is usually intended to represent an aquatic insect nearing its final stage of development, the stretching and drying of wings. It should be noted, however, that some 'dry' patterns are tied to mimic the spent fly after mating and egg laying has taken place. Others are designed to cover the various terrestrial insects that are blown onto the surface of the water at various times during the year, hawthorn flies, crane flies, flying ants, etc. Both the spent fly patterns and terrestrial imitations should be tied to fish slightly deeper in the surface film, but more on that subject later.

What the Fish Sees

In one aspect at least, dry fly fishing is no different to any other kind of angling. Presentation is everything.

In order to deceive the trout the fly must look very similar to the natural insect on which it is feeding. You will notice I said similar, not exactly. It's just not possible to tie an *exact* replica. We're not that clever. Besides, what the trout sees and what we see are two quite different things. And that is why, at this point, we would do well to consider what our quarry regards as natural when they begin taking insects from the surface.

In the first place the fish see a shape, probably no more than a rough outline of a certain colour, suspended above a row of dots or depressions caused by the insect's feet and legs as it stands on the skin of the water. Consequently, any good imitation must be capable of supporting itself in a similar fashion without additional assistance. This effect can be achieved solely by the use of good quality hackle feathers during the construction of the fly. It is on the points of this feather that the fly will stand. The application of commercial floatants to improve buoyancy should only be necessary in the roughest of conditions. Even then it is a practice I avoid if at all possible.

Some people also like to grease the leader to help keep the fly afloat. But this too is flirting with danger. When the trout looks up at the real thing it does not expect to see a length of attached nylon floating on the surface. This is particularly off-putting in flat calm conditions when even the finest of leaders must seem like the tow rope of a North Sea tug boat to the fish.

So what about colour? The eye of a fish is essentially different in its make up to that of humans and it sees colours quite differently. Having said that it is not something we should worry too much about. Providing we can match the shape and the shade of the hatching insect it matters little to the angler whether yellow appears green to the trout, or whether in fact black appears blue!

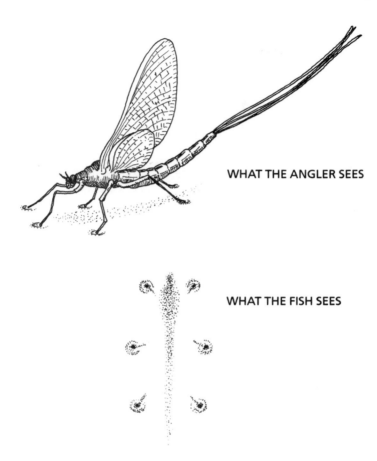

WHAT THE ANGLER SEES

WHAT THE FISH SEES

Right Time – Right Place – Right Fly

To achieve the best results from the dry fly it makes sense to restrict its use to those times when the fish can be seen taking adult insects from the surface. That is not to say that a trout cannot sometimes be tempted up from the depths to take a dry pattern. Of course it can. But I'm a great believer in presenting the fly at the depth at which the fish are feeding. If they're tucking into bloodworm on the bottom, that's where you'll find my fly. By the same token if they're sipping down adult mayflies from the surface then my artificial will be up there amongst them.

Unfortunately it is not always easy to determine the exact depth at which feeding is taking place even when most of the activity is going on near the surface. Perhaps the best advice I can give you under the circumstances is simply to watch carefully. The softer, 'bulging' rise

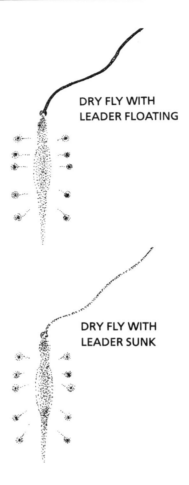

DRY FLY WITH
LEADER FLOATING

DRY FLY WITH
LEADER SUNK

forms are usually caused by fish taking nymphs in, or just under, the surface film. The splashier rises tend to occur when the insects are being taken right off the top. It's these you need to watch for. That's a very rough guide I know but with practice you'll be surprised at how accurate your judgement can become. And if uncertain you can always do the obvious. Try a nymph to begin with and if this is unsuccessful put up a dry fly. What have you got to lose?

Once you have established that the fish are feeding on surface flies your next step must be to identify the species. This is not quite as difficult as it might sound for a small percentage always survive the attentions of the trout and will be heading for the bank. Invariably you will find a number of them fluttering around the margins or clinging to bank-side vegetation. There are only three major families of aquatic insects that are likely to generate prolonged surface activity so a degree in entomology isn't necessary. Having said that, however, it's important that the angler is able to tell the difference between a midge, a sedge and a mayfly. And so, for that purpose, here is a brief description of the three species I'm referring to.

Chironomidae: Midges (Buzzers)
Body appears hook shaped in the nymphal state. Referred to as 'buzzers' by anglers because of the sound made by their wings in flight. Probably the most ubiquitous of all water-born insects. Common across the whole of the British Isles. They can bite like Count Dracula and around the larger Scottish lochs have been known to drive even the animals to distraction. Most buzzers are eaten by the fish in the larval (bloodworm) or nymphal stages of development but during a heavy hatch sufficient flies will reach the surface to provoke the kind of response dry fly anglers will be looking for.

Ephemeroptera: Mayflies
Body soft, antennae short, abdomen long terminating in three cerci (tails), four membranous transparent wings, held upright when at rest. A pretty, rather elegant family of flies, easily identified by the upswept wing position and long, arched body. Unique in the fact that the initial metamorphosis from nymph to winged insect is not the final stage of hatching. In this intermediate state the fly is known as a sub-imago or, to anglers, a 'dun'. This common name derives from the creature's dull olive/brown colour. After reaching bank-side vegetation it rests. Shortly afterwards a second moult takes place, revealing the adult mayfly, or 'spinner'.

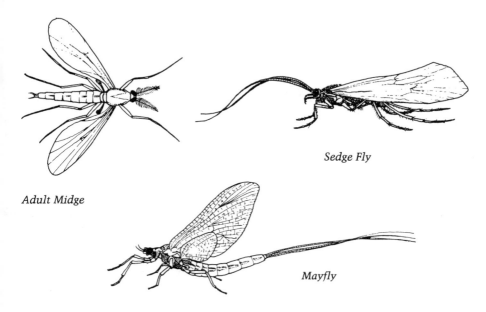

Sedge Fly

Adult Midge

Mayfly

Trichoptera: Sedge flies

Moth-like insects with membranous and hairy wings held roof-wise when at rest. There are many sub-species of this family of insects that hatch out during daylight hours, but they seem to hold little interest for the trout. It is the larger, paler flies that usually appear at dusk that are likely to generate a prolific rise from the fish. Sedges are clumsy fliers, requiring something of a 'run up' before leaving the water and taking to the air.

Tactics

Many stillwater anglers underestimate the value of dry fly fishing, probably because they have only dabbled with it and it has not rewarded them with immediate results. In other words, they've not been serious about it. And let's face it, throwing out a lure or a wet fly of some sort and whizzing it back mid-water is always likely to produce a few fish if that's all you're looking for. But that kind of lackadaisical attitude won't do if you intend to try for success with a dry fly. Using imitative patterns has always required a far more thoughtful and delicate approach, never more so than with true surface fishing. And so, for those of you who are interested, let's get on and look at the practicalities of fishing a dry fly.

I'd like to begin by asking you to imagine that we have already discovered a few fish feeding on hatching olive duns. They are within comfortable casting range from the bank and so reaching them won't be a problem. And we have no doubts as to the species of fly the fish are taking. There is enough of a breeze to create a slight ripple but not enough to disguise the profile of the insects on the water. Those upright wings, like the sails of a tiny boat, tell us all too clearly that these are of the Ephemeroptera family. Besides, a significant number are already fluttering amongst the bushes and reeds along the bank.

Our tackle at this point should consist of a rod with a fairly gentle action, a No. 7 floating line and a leader of at least eighteen feet graduated down to a point of no more than 3 lb breaking strain. This may seem light to you, particularly if most of your fishing to date has been with lures on leaders of 5–6 lb breaking strain. Nevertheless, don't be tempted into using something heavier. Even fine nylon can be spotted quite easily by the fish when it's lying on the surface. The thicker stuff must look like clothes line!

Our next decision must be what fly to use. Given the conditions described earlier I would probably plump for a Lake Olive, size 12, one with a nice stiff hackle that would make it ride high in the water.

Our last act (and to my mind one of the most important) before making the cast should be to thoroughly de-grease the last yard of leader. That is the three feet nearest the fly. The logic behind this move is fairly obvious when you cast your mind back to the earlier paragraph on what the fish sees. The nylon attached to the fly is far less conspicuous below the surface than when floating on the top. In fact in flat calm conditions I'm quite prepared to sink the whole leader rather than risk spooking the fish. Today though, with that forgiving ripple, perhaps a yard will be sufficient.

There are only two things to keep in mind when the cast is made. First, we should try to put the fly down as gently as possible, and secondly, we should never disturb the trout by casting too far and dropping the heavy fly line itself over their position – this is known as 'lining' the fish. Putting the fly down lightly can be achieved quite simply by aiming high, making sure that the line straightens fully before the fly hits the water. This causes a slight recoil that stops the fly dead in mid-air, allowing it to fall parachute fashion.

In my experience the first twenty seconds after the fly has alighted on the water are the most critical to the angler. The longer it sits there after that the more likely it is to remain unmolested. This is especially true when the cast is made into a general area of activity rather than to an individually cruising fish. It seems to me that the trout make up their minds very quickly. The fly appears in their window and in that split second they either decide to take it and do so, or they ignore it altogether. One thing is certain. The longer they look the less likely they are to take. As a consequence I'm not one of those anglers who will sit all afternoon watching their dry fly bobbing around the pool. If it is not devoured by a fish inside half a minute I lift off and re-cast.

I've lost count of the number of times my fly has settled on the water and a trout has immediately appeared alongside it, seemingly intent on a good meal. Yet at the last second it turns up its nose and glides away again. This can be very frustrating. But in its own way it is no different to the frustrations suffered by a river angler in a similar situation. Anyone who fishes running water regularly will tell you of times when they covered a rising trout with a dry fly again and again, and although

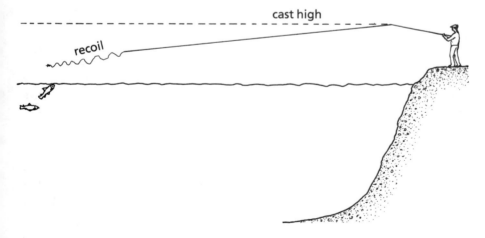

Deliver the dry fly softly: cast high and allow the line to recoil.

the fish will often inspect the fly closely, it usually stops short of actually eating it. Then, a cast or two later – for reasons best known to itself that same fish will rise and take the same fly as if it had been waiting for it all day.

Now, back to the fishing. Imagine if you would that the cast has been made. We've managed to pull the fly up short in mid-air as suggested earlier and it has just floated gently down and settled on the surface. Then, as we watch, a good fish appears just beneath it. How do they do that, just appear in that fashion? They seem to rise up like a submarine blowing its ballast tanks. The water is empty one moment, a second later you are aware of a long, grey shape that has simply materialized. This one nudges the fly but turns away again. Never mind. We lift off and try once more.

The hole in the water into which the fly fell is actually an optical illusion caused by the trout sucking it down. We are slightly surprised at the speed of it all. The fly didn't even have a chance to settle properly before it was taken. The only danger now is that panic will take a hand, causing us to over-react and strike wildly, forgetting momentarily that fragile 3 lb breaking strain point connecting us to the fish. But there really is no need to rush. In fact a short delay in the angler's response can be quite beneficial. Traditional dry fly anglers were encouraged to recite, 'God Save the Queen' between rising a trout and striking into it. This was supposed to ensure that the fish actually had the hook in its mouth and was turning away before tension was applied to the line. I won't ask you to do that. I would, however, suggest a slight pause, possibly long enough for a deep breath to help steady the nerves. During this brief period of waiting you might even be lucky enough to notice the tip of the line drawing away from you, a wonderful sight to any angler.

When it comes to striking into the fish please do so circumspectly. Lifting the rod tip is usually enough to set the hook. There's no need for anything more violent than that. It's worth remembering that anything too vigorous is likely to snap that fine point and undo all your good work.

You may have noticed by now that at no time have I suggested moving the fly after the cast has been made. I am aware that this is fairly common practice amongst many stillwater anglers but to my mind it always smacks a little of desperation. What usually happens is that the fly is delivered into the area of activity but is ignored by the fish. The angler, losing patience after a minute or so, then decides to twitch the fly across the surface in the hope of provoking a chase from some hungry trout. The fact that this sometimes happens owes more to the naivety of the fish than the tactic itself. The truth is that it is almost impossible to move the fly across the surface in a lifelike manner, no matter how hard we try. That twenty or twenty-five yards of line separating you from the business end of your tackle is a wonderful sponge for absorbing and distorting delicate movement. A pull of two or three inches doesn't even take the kinks out of the line, while something more energetic moves the fly at a quite unrealistic speed.

But, if left alone, the action of wind and wave will impart some life to the fly, probably a far more natural movement than anything the angler can achieve.

If you do happen to find yourself in that happy position when the trout are prepared to chase your dry fly across the top on a regular basis, then don't bother with a dry fly at all! Switch to a Muddler pattern, or even a Spider, and pull this through just sub-surface. You'll find the offers coming even more frequently.

Having spent the last five minutes or so advising you against moving your fly after casting, there are a couple of exceptions to this basic rule that I should like to touch upon.

When describing earlier the three major families of insects likely to generate lasting surface activity, I suggested sedge flies were clumsy fliers that required a 'run up' to get airborne. This take-off procedure, known to most experienced anglers as 'skittering', excites the trout to the point when they will pursue the fly for some distance across the surface before devouring it. Under those conditions it makes sense for anglers to try copying the behaviour of the natural. And to be honest, it's a wonderfully exciting method to use – seeing that bow wave appear just behind the fly as you begin moving it, then the sudden surge before the line goes 'heavy'.

The second exception to my basic 'no movement' rule applies to flies that are designed to be fished partially submerged. In the strict sense these are not dry flies at all as they sit *in* the surface film rather than *on* it. For further details on this topic see the next chapter on 'Fishing the film'.

Before leaving the subject of dry fly fishing altogether I'd like to say a few words on the subject of artificial floatants. My dislike of bottles and sprays full of chemicals is purely personal. Having said that I would like to believe it is a mistrust that is also based upon logic and reason.

For instance, I haven't yet come across a commercial compound that doesn't have a smell of some kind to it. I must be honest and say that, for fear of poisoning myself, I haven't actually tasted one yet. I suspect if I had done so that the flavour wouldn't have been particularly pleasant. And on that basis alone I'm reluctant to cover my flies with it. Besides, if I can tie patterns that will float unassisted, why should I take the risk of making them less appealing to the trout by tainting them unnaturally?

I dislike greased leaders quite simply because floating nylon is much more likely to spook the fish than nylon lying an inch down in the surface film. It is true that floating leaders become less obvious when the water surface is broken or agitated by a vigorous ripple, but even then I would never advocate the use of excessive greasing. However, if the occasion should arise when you feel that your leader is sinking so quickly that it is in danger of drowning your fly, here's a tip I was given many years ago that will overcome the problem. Merely rub the tips of your fingers across your forehead and down the planes of your face. In doing so you will have collected more than enough natural grease from the skin for the necessary application. It's a case of a little going a long way.

FISHING THE FILM

GENERAL ADVICE

I can think of very few more galling experiences for the fly fisher than those occasions during the warmer months of the year when, although fish can be seen taking flies from the surface, they refuse steadfastly to look at any artificial that is offered. To cover water where we suspect fish might be and to receive no offers is bad enough. But to be faced with trout feeding like ladies let loose in a chocolate factory, and to have every one of our immaculately prepared and presented flies ignored, it's enough to drive even the most reasonable amongst us to distraction.

Has it happened to me? Yes, many times, as it must have happened to you. And now it breaks my heart to think of how often I allowed that situation to get the better of me before I actually began thinking the problem through. Let me give you some idea of how I used to react so that you can compare my tactics with your own.

It's a warm dull morning, overcast and very still. I haven't gone very far along the bank when, clever old me, I spot rising fish. Not just one or two but quite a number. Scared someone else might beat me to it I break into a trot and am relieved when I reach the most favourable spot first. I begin fishing with my favourite Nymph, flinging it out and waiting a second or two before twitching it seductively back, just twelve inches down. At any moment I expect that lovely long draw on the line that signals a taking fish and I'm quite surprised when nothing happens. Never mind. There's time yet. I stick with that Nymph for another ten minutes before trying a change of fly, a similar pattern but much smaller.

Ten more unsuccessful minutes go by and the doubts begin to creep in. What about a Buzzer Nymph? Brilliant! That should do the trick. On go a team of Buzzers, red on the point, black on the first dropper, green on the second. But my patience is running thin by this time and half a dozen casts later I'm back rummaging in my fly box for something out of the ordinary. Twenty five minutes have passed and already I've stopped thinking!

It's desperation tactics now, a change of fly every cast. There are creations coming out of my box that might have been designed by Salvador Dali after a heavy night on Stilton cheese and red wine. But the fish are not in the least impressed. They continue to behave as if I didn't exist. I'm now just about at the end of my tether. But there's one more thing I can try before I'm done: something big and hairy fished at speed just below the surface. On goes the biggest Muddler I own. I cast it roughly in the direction where most of the activity is taking place and begin ripping it back as soon as it hits the water. Result? It makes my arms ache!

Sounds familiar? Depressingly so, I suspect. But could I have done anything other than that which I did? After all, I put the effort in, and my intentions were good. Unfortunately, good intentions plus effort don't always equate to success in angling. A little less effort and a lot more thought might have helped me solve the problem a deal quicker than I eventually did.

I have always prided myself on having a fairly logical mind and solving a problem gives me enormous pleasure. To adopt a reasoned and methodical approach to a given set of circumstances, then to arrive at a conclusion that proves to be correct, is no small triumph for the thinking man. It is a fact, however, that before a problem can be solved it is first necessary that it be fully understood. At least that was what I thought at the time. Sadly, in the context of angling, this is not always possible. Take the situation we have just talked about. I could see the fish feeding near the surface, but didn't know on what, or even if my flies were a reasonable imitation. The only indisputable fact was that the trout found them, and my presentation, unacceptable.

What then could I do to come to grips with conditions such as these? To be perfectly frank I was at a loss as to know what to do. In the end, and after a great deal of thought, I did the only thing possible. I took an educated guess! If this seems a slightly risky ploy to you then put yourself in my position: what else could I have done?

It was some years later before I discovered that my chosen method for solving this problem was in fact a common practice in laboratories all over the world. I happened to be talking to another angler – a science teacher at a well-known school – who explained that solutions to scientific problems are often found without every facet being first understood. As he put it, 'We take what knowledge we have and use it to make an educated guess. Then we calculate what the end result should be. After that we set about testing our educated guess. And if the results of the test agree with our calculations it is reasonable to assume that we are right!' Easy when it's put like that, isn't it?

In this case my 'educated guess' was based upon the evidence of my own eyes, plus a goodly number of years' experience in trying to persuade trout to take an artificial fly. I was convinced that the fish to which I was casting were actually feeding and not 'sporting' as they sometimes do, particularly rainbows. But if they were feeding, yet were not at all interested in what I offered them, what was I doing wrong? Could it be the pattern of fly I was offering? Possibly, but I had my doubts. One thing I had noticed during those difficult periods of fish activity, only a minimal number of insects seemed to be hatching, and these on the whole were very small. There was also quite a mixture of species. And the way the trout were feeding didn't suggest a vigorous hatch of fly – there was nothing frenzied about it, it was a fairly leisurely business.

I can't remember exactly what it was that set me off on the right path but I suspect it was this awareness of the very small size of the hatching insect. But there had to be more to it than that. I began to search my mind for other anomalies that might help and then remembered that, more often than not, the conditions that seemed to encourage the trout to feed in this fashion were warm days with little or no wind, when the surface film must be at its thickest.

I think it was at this point that the penny finally dropped. A variety of tiny, feeble insects working their way up through the water, and then coming into contact with that final sticky, glutinous barrier? It was no wonder that the fish could afford to feed leisurely. There was no quick escape route for the hatching flies. Those lucky enough to make it through to the surface would only do so after a prolonged period of effort. Some would not make it at all. They would die there, literally drowned, only inches from salvation.

These then were the conditions that caused me such heartache. At least, that was how I'd worked it out. The proof of the pudding would of course be in the eating. If I could devise a small, general fly pattern that was acceptable to the fish, and then learn to fish it in a lifelike way up in the surface film? Well, who knows what might happen!

The fly I settled on was a tiny Spider pattern and, in order not to confuse the issue too much, I tied them in just two colours, olive green and yellow. I christened them later, 'Summer Spiders'. They were tied on hook sizes 12/14/16.

I didn't have to wait long to test out my theories. A medium sized lake not far from my home was renowned as a difficult summer venue for exactly the reasons we have just discussed. It was a place not noted for prolific insect life, yet there always seemed to be some flies coming off, albeit they were small and the hatches sparse. About the nearest thing they ever got to a decent hatch of flies would be a modest showing of tiny pond olives, about the smallest I'd ever seen.

For several days I did nothing but watch the weather. Then, on a warm overcast afternoon, I set about putting my ideas to the test. Conditions couldn't have been better. The lake when I arrived was like a mill pond and there were enough anglers with long faces around the banks to tell me that I'd chosen the perfect day. The trout were being just as difficult as I'd hoped.

I decided to fish from a spot where a short promontory jutted out into the water. There was no shortage of targets to aim at. The surface of the pool may not have been alive with fish but there was plenty of evidence of the sort of sub-surface activity I'd been hoping for, with regular 'bulging' rises in most areas.

I suppose I was lucky in that this activity seemed to increase somewhat soon after my arrival. Having said that, however, no other anglers were enjoying success at the time. I put up an Olive Spider, size 14, to a point of 3 lb breaking strain, making sure the leader was fully de-greased before casting. Then, after wetting the fly thoroughly, I was about to make a start when two fish rose in front of me, just a couple of yards apart. Not knowing which of them to cast at I did the next best thing and dropped the Spider between them.

My line, a good quality floater, was riding nice and high in the water. I straightened it carefully and waited a couple of seconds for the fly and the first yard of leader to sink into the film, then began my retrieve with a gentle pull of about eight inches. Quick as a wink the line twitched. Without thinking I lifted the rod tip and was fast into the fish. I was astonished. I'd hoped for success, but first throw? That had been too much to expect.

The story of the rest of that afternoon was of an eight fish limit on a day when the next best result was three, and that from someone who'd been at the waterside since first light. Obviously not all the fish came to the very first pull on the retrieve. Some followed the fly for some distance before being overcome and grabbing hold. But in all cases the take occurred after the fly had been allowed to sink just an inch or so and then was retrieved very gently. I realized later that this was probably causing the spider to climb at a shallow angle towards the surface in a most lifelike fashion. In addition the soft hen hackle I'd used when tying the fly would be opening and closing like an umbrella as it travelled through the water, enhancing the overall animation.

I learned something else too that afternoon, but not until I'd taken the fly away from the pursuing fish on at least six occasions. It can be a nerve-racking business fishing these tiny patterns just under the surface, particularly when a heavy bow wave appears a few inches behind the fly, caused as the trout slides up to investigate. Give the line a pull and the Spider climbs gently to the surface, then the bow wave appears as the fish closes in. The problem is that it doesn't always grab hold at that point. Strike in anticipation, as I did, and you're simply taking the fly away from the fish. If you cannot control your nerves at this crucial stage you'd do far better to look away and wait for the line to go 'heavy', which is what usually happens when the fish takes hold. For those of you who have the will-power to watch the whole sequence through to its conclusion you will notice that, in the split second before the fly is taken, the bow wave disappears as the trout puts its head down prior to taking the fly from beneath.

Spent Flies

Adult insects that have come to the end of their useful lives and have fallen exhausted onto the water are easy prey for the trout. This often involves quite large numbers of fly, especially after a heavy mayfly hatch. Needless to say the fish soon cotton on to this additional supply of protein and it's a common enough sight to see them mopping up the tiny corpses in a very relaxed and stately fashion.

There have been times when they've reminded me of dolphins, the way they head and tail through the water, totally preoccupied as they gorge themselves at this unexpected banquet.

Logically, catching these fish should not pose too great a problem for anglers. And yet, having said that, some fly fishers still fail to make the most of a situation like this. Many have admitted to me that they experienced difficulty in persuading the trout to take their offerings. Indeed, on some occasions, failing to rise even a single fish!

After some debate it became clear that more often than not the reason for their failure was that few of them actually fished with a 'spent' pattern. They relied instead upon a true dry fly, which doesn't actually mimic the condition of the natural insect at that moment in time.

It is important to realize that the spent fly does not sit up perkily as it did when newly hatched. It tends to lie upon, or partially submerged within, the surface film, depending upon how long it has been in the water. To achieve this condition an artificial must be tied with a much sparser hackle, one that allows the body, and in particular the wings, of the fly to come into contact with the water surface.

From a personal point of view I made a breakthrough with my own version of a spent fly after discovering the flat polyfoam mentioned earlier (see the discussion on the Flying Ant in the August chapter). It is wonderful material for winging spent patterns and, being buoyant, permits the fly to be tied with a very sparse hackle. When on the water it looks just like the real thing. The spread wings support the spindly legs and the rest of the body perfectly. And there is the added advantage that, even with the leader de-greased (still very important), this fly will sit in the surface film all day, exactly where it should be.

My tactics for fishing this pattern are pretty well the same as for fishing any dry fly, with the exception that I am happy to leave it much longer in the water. I would still be reluctant to use a point of more than 3 lb breaking strain and, as stated earlier, consider the sinking of at least part of the leader to be essential.

Casting to Cruising Fish

Before finally leaving the subject of surface fishing I'd like to touch briefly upon those occasions when a solitary fish can be seen cruising and feeding in the upper water layers. Individual fish activity in these rainbow dominated days is, I find, something of a rarity. Shoal activity is much more common and I have always preached the gospel that if you can find one rainbow you'll most likely have found a dozen or so.

There are, however, exceptions to the rule, fish that for some reason have taken up a more monastic lifestyle. I've never been able to resist the challenge that these 'lone rangers' represent. They are inevitably more difficult to tempt than a fish within a shoal, competing with others for what is on offer. And of course they are not influenced by shoal behaviour, when the response of one hungry trout will often trigger off a feeding spree amongst the others.

To my mind there are few more engrossing forms of fishing than the pursuit of an individual fish. It is a very personal thing, a 'one on one' situation that never fails to excite me. It is quite different from casting a fly into water where you know that any one of a dozen hungry trout are likely to grab hold. That, enjoyable and satisfying though it might be, is not quite the same.

Although I have been an angler since the age of seven, some things never change. Whenever I see a solitary fish busily working one particular stretch of water, when I can track its movements from the rise forms caused as it forages for titbits in the surface film, when I have put my fly in its path and am waiting for a reaction, my heart still hammers and my hands sweat like a novice's. And if I am lucky enough to persuade that fish to take my fly, well . . . it's as though I'd reached out a hand and simply plucked it from the water. The hair on the back of my neck prickles just thinking about it.

Alright Musgrove, that's enough daydreaming. Back to business.

The fly I prefer for this sort of fishing is an old favourite of mine, a size 10 Suspender Buzzer. This is a buzzer pattern with a small ball of plastazote or some other buoyant material tied in at its head, just enough to suspend it within the surface film. As to the colour, I find that red, black, green, brown and orange are sufficient to cover most eventualities. I usually fish it as I would the spent fly with one important exception. After spotting my quarry and establishing the general direction of its route, I make the cast nice and early, well in front of the fish. That gives me time to straighten the line and settle myself in preparation for what is to come. What I'm actually doing is setting a trap. If my luck is in and Mr Trout continues swimming and feeding along the same line, I wait until he is within a yard or so of the fly . . . and then I move it! Not excessively – I simply lift the rod tip a couple of feet. This causes the buzzer to wriggle sideways, almost breaking the surface, and is usually enough to provoke a response from the fish. If everything works out as planned there will be a gentle boil, followed by a gradual tightening of the line that signifies the fish has taken the fly and is turning away.

Things don't always work out as planned of course. It wouldn't be fishing if they did. On countless occasions, having taken infinite pains to work out the route that a fish was taking, I've put out my fly only to find that the ungrateful trout has done a quick about-turn and gone shooting off in the opposite direction, leaving me cursing under my breath. But when things *do* go right . . . when it all comes together as if by magic . . . ah, that really is a moment to savour.

TWO FLIES FOR FISHING THE FILM

The Summer Spider

Tying Instructions

HOOK: Partridge Grey Shadow GRS3A, size 12/14/16.
THREAD: Green/black/yellow/orange.

THORAX: Seal's fur substitute.
TAIL: Hen hackle fibres.
HACKLE: Soft hen (the softer the better).
RIB: Fine brass or copper wire.

Wind the tying thread in nice tight touching coils down the shank of the hook from eye to bend, tying in the rib as you go. Remember that the thread will represent the body of the fly, so neatness is important at this stage. When the bend of the hook is reached tie in a few longer hackle fibres as a tail before taking the thread back towards the eye, once again in neat turns. This second layer of silk should stop short of the eye, occupying about two-thirds of the hook shank, leaving room for the thorax and hackle. Now wind on the rib. Follow this by dubbing on the sparsest possible thorax, which should be no more than a few wisps, then finish off with a nice soft hackle. Two turns is plenty, three too much!

The Spent Mayfly

Tying Instructions

HOOK: Partridge Yorkshire K10, size 12/14.
THREAD: Yellow.
WINGS: Flat polyfoam.
TAIL: Three cock pheasant tail fibres.
HACKLE: Neutral cock.

The specialized double shank of this particular hook pattern requires a slightly different approach from the usual straight 'down and up' style of fly-tying. Begin with the hook clamped in the vice with the eye pointing to the right, (the usual position). Then take the thread in neat, touching turns down the double shank as far as the hook bend. At this point (where the shank splits) swivel the hook position in the vice to give yourself better access and continue winding on the silk along the upper, curved section of the hook that forms the body extension. At this juncture you can tie in the tail of the fly, just three cock pheasant tail fibres, as you work your way to the end of the body extension. Having done that, return the thread to where this section meets the hook bend and, once more, reverse the hook so that the eye is again pointing to the right – fiddly, I know, but good access is important. Lay down another half dozen coils of silk over the double shank, then leave the thread hanging there on the bobbin holder. This gives you both hands free for the winging. From a sheet of flat polyfoam cut the wings to shape and tie them carefully in position (upright or extended). Finish off with a sparse hackle.

CONCLUSION – THAT VITAL INGREDIENT

If I was asked to identify a single quality that might transform a poor angler into a good one it would have to be enthusiasm. Without enthusiasm nothing lasting or worthwhile can be achieved. My mother, like most mothers, had an adage of some kind for all occasions. On the subject of enthusiasm she would say: 'Son, the world is full of tired Tims and weary Willies. I *don't* want you turning out like them!' She's been dead now for many years but whenever I repeat those words to myself I suddenly see her face looking down at me, and her finger, like a pistol barrel, pointing in my direction.

Hers was good advice, the best, and I've tried to instill the same values into my own children. I found it therefore slightly paradoxical when I realized that the excessive enthusiasm fuelling the fires of most dedicated anglers, driving them on in their pursuit of the fish, could sometimes also be their Achilles' heel – in fact, a positive drawback! To help you understand the point I'm trying to make let me quote to you from the dictionary lying open in front of me on my desk. It defines the word 'fanatical' as 'excessively enthusiastic'!

And there you have it. Those of us who think of little else but the pursuit and capture of the fish are in fact fanatics. The drawback to being a fanatic is that our enthusiasm rarely allows us to step back far enough from what we're involved in at any particular moment to take a detached look at the whole picture. 'Can't see the wood for the trees' is another old saying that springs to mind.

And so let me re-state my case. Enthusiasm is a vital ingredient in the making of a successful angler. But it should be allied to calm and rational thought – that's the real secret. Unfortunately all too often enthusiasm is permitted to take over and, when straight thinking goes out of the window, so do your chances of success. How many times have you gone home from a day's fishing cursing your luck because the fates seem to have conspired against you? And yet in the peace and quiet of your sitting room – with a full stomach and in a pensive frame of mind – when the day's events are recalled all too clearly, you then begin to recognize those signs you should have recognized at the waterside earlier, the clues that were pointing out the direction you should have taken had you the vision to see. Sadly the twin blindfolds of excitement and enthusiasm are rarely lifted from our eyes until too late.

This train of thought began just a few days ago when I found myself sharing a stretch of bank at the Draycote Fishery near Rugby with twenty or so other anglers. It was a cold day and a heavy wind was pushing two foot waves from the dam end of the reservoir down into the Toft Shallows area where I was fishing. It was an unpleasant day. The only good thing to be said was that at least the wind was left to right, perfect for orthodox casters.

The trouble started when, after a deadly dull period of inactivity, one angler (wearing the brightest red sweater I think I've ever seen) took three fish in three casts on a Cat's Whisker pulled through very fast at mid-water level. 'He's on a Cat's Whisker' – the word went up and down the bank and hurried changes were made. Unconvinced, I resisted the temptation, deciding instead to keep faith in my large, leaded Nymph, at least until something more conclusive happened.

Twenty Cat's Whiskers went whistling out into the lake, and twenty Cat's Whiskers were retrieved fast at mid-water. The trout, sensibly, ignored them. Out and back, out and back went the flies – anglers grim faced and determined, risking wet feet as they strove for that extra yard of distance, the waves slapping hard against the tops of their waders.

No other fish were taken during the next thirty minutes. Even the man in the hunting pink sweater, the one who'd started all the activity, failed to produce any more. Not that we stopped trying. The flies were still being hurled out and pulled back frantically. It was as if all those anglers had been programmed. It had worked once, it *must* work again.

Sadly, my own Nymph was proving just as unattractive to the trout. I was actually considering switching from my floating line to an intermediate or slow sinker with a lure of some kind, but decided instead to stop for coffee. Taking a break like this has helped me on innumerable occasions. It's not that I need the drink, I just need time to think. The coffee is merely an excuse.

I was sitting there on a large rock, chilled and slightly dejected, peering out at the water, day-dreaming rather than looking, when I saw a fin appear in the trough between the waves. I didn't believe it of course. I was convinced my eyes were playing tricks on me. But two seconds later another fish head and tailed in one of the million smooth valleys of water between wave caps, and this time I was sure.

I could have laughed when I thought about it. The trout were up on the surface and we were all fishing underneath them, scraping their bellies with our flies. My leaded Nymph was probably not much shallower than the lures that were being fished by the others that day. We had all allowed ourselves to be influenced by the first three fish caught and had stopped thinking. And even though our tactics proved to be flawed we still pressed on casting and retrieving like automatons. Certainly the fish were difficult to spot with two foot waves rolling down the length of the fishery, but the truth was that no one had really looked. When finally I spotted them, by accident as it were, they were easy enough to see. And the more I looked the more I saw.

Sport for me from that moment on was fabulous. I found a few buzzers in the water at my feet, large orange ones. A couple of size 10 artificials to a 3½lb breaking strain point brought me an offer every cast and in no time I had taken my eight fish limit.

Strangely, the people on either side of me continued to throw out their lures as if convinced that by will-power alone they could persuade the fish to come to their flies. That's enthusiasm for you.

I had six fish on the bank before the chap next door came to ask how I was doing it. Even then it took a minute or so to convince him that the fish really were up on the surface. Fortunately there were still enough showing for me to be able to point them out to him. And of course once he'd seen one he immediately saw a dozen.

I'm happy to say that when I left a little while later almost every angler was using a floating line and Buzzers, and enough rods were bending into trout to suggest that a few more limit bags would be taken before that day was over.

I have not gone to the trouble of repeating that story simply to sing my own praises. God knows I've been caught out more than most over the years. The point I'm trying to make is that going through the motions of fishing merely for the sake of it is a waste of time and energy. The act of casting and retrieving can be extremely seductive on its own – feeling the rod working in the hand, watching the line slide out over the water like a snake – but fishing without thought is a largely useless exercise. And if you find yourself ever reaching the stage where you're thinking of something else rather than how to catch your fish, then stop! Take a break. Put down your rod and leave it for a while. Have a coffee and a sandwich. It's at that point your mind will begin to work for you again and, with luck, a sensible strategy be formed.

INDEX